THE LIBERAL PROJECT AND THE TRANSFORMATION OF DEMOCRACY

Eugenia and Hugh M. Stewart '26 Series on Eastern Europe
Stjepan Meštrović, *General Editor*

THE LIBERAL PROJECT AND THE TRANSFORMATION OF DEMOCRACY

The Case of East Central Europe

SABRINA P. RAMET

Texas A&M University Press, College Station

♾ ♻

Library of Congress Cataloging-in-Publication Data

Ramet, Sabrina P., 1949–
    The liberal project and the transformaton of deomocracy : the case of East Central
    Europe / Sabrina P. Ramet.
        p.   cm. — (Eugenia and Hugh M. Stewart '26 series on Eastern Europe)
    Includes bibliographical references and index.
    ISBN-13: 978-1-58544-575-2 (cloth : alk. paper)
    ISBN-10: 1-58544-575-4 (cloth : alk. paper)
    ISBN-13: 978-1-58544-579-0 (pbk. : alk. paper)
    ISBN-10: 1-58544-579-7 (pbk. : alk. paper)
 1. Europe, Eastern—Politics and government—1989– . 2. Liberalism—Europe,
Eastern. 3. Democracy—Europe, Eastern. I. Title.
    DJK51.R348 2007
    320.9437—dc22
                                                            2006021787

To Pallas Athena, Goddess of Wisdom
and Protectrix of Democracy,
and
To Jim Sadkovich, friend

CONTENTS

PREFACE

I t is my hope that this volume reaches a readership wider than the field of East European studies. Although most of my examples are taken from the East European context (with those not from Eastern Europe having been drawn from the contemporary United States), I believe that the framework developed here may have a more general applicability. Certainly the issues of democratization, liberalism, capitalism, gender equality, the claims of nationalism, and policy debates sparked by religious faith are common to all continents, and the challenges they present have nowhere been satisfactorily resolved. Indeed, in countries once thought to be paragons of stable liberal democracy, the old formulae have been subverted and local publics have become more polarized than they had been in a century or more.

With the exception of chapters 2, 6, and 8, earlier versions of all the chapters included here have been published previously, whether in whole or in part; all of them have, however, been revised for republication here—some of them extensively. Chapter 5 was first published in *Human Rights Review* 2, no. 1 (2000): 84–103. Chapters 1, 3, 4, and 9 were first published as "Eastern Europe and the Natural Law Tradition," *Donald W. Treadgold Papers in Russian, East European, and Central Asian Studies,* no. 27 (Seattle: HMJ School of International Studies Russian and East European Studies Program, August 2000). Chapter 7 was first published in Serbian translation under the title "Klizanje unazad: Sudbina žena u centralnoj i istočnoj Evropi posle

1989," in *Ljudska bezbednost/Human Security* (Belgrade) 1, no. 1 (2003): 115–33. The first English publication of chapter 7 was "Sliding Backwards: The Fate of Women in Post-1989 East-Central Europe," published online by *Kakanien Revisited* (December 2004), at www.kakanien.ac.at/beitr/fallstudie/Sramet.pdf. I am grateful to these journals, editors, and publishers for permission to reissue these works in revised format.

I began work on this book while I was still teaching at the University of Washington, continued after I took up a new post at the Norwegian University of Science and Technology (NTNU) in Trondheim, Norway, and completed it during the 2005/6 academic year, during which time I have enjoyed access to the holdings (both paper and electronic) at Georgetown University (as Visiting Researcher) and at the Woodrow Wilson International Center for Scholars (as Senior Policy Fellow). I also wish to thank the Peace Research Institute, Oslo, where I am a Senior Associate, for its support. I am grateful to Ola Listhaug for his support of my research and for his assistance in solving critical problems as they have arisen, to Beata Eggan, Krystof Koseła, and Maryjane Osa for putting me in touch with appropriate persons during my summer 2004 research trip to Poland (which contributed to the research for chapter 6), to Stefano Bianchini, whose invitation to present a lecture at Bertinoro in September 2003 inspired me to write chapter 7, to Jonathon Moses for his helpful feedback on chapter 8, and, as ever, to Christine Hassenstab, my spouse, for her enthusiasm for my work and for the intellectual discourse we enjoy. I also wish to thank Łukasz Kocan, my Polish tutor, for checking the diacritics on Polish names, and György Péteri, my friend and NTNU colleague, for checking the diacritics on Hungarian names. I am also grateful to Charles King and Angela Stent for arranging for my visiting appointment to Georgetown University, to Jennifer Long, Andy Pino, and Sissel Tramposch for practical assistance while at Georgetown, to Marty Sletzinger and Michael Van Dusen for arranging for my visiting appointment to the Wilson Center, and to Dagne Gizaw, Michelle Kamalich, and Janet Spikes for practical assistance via the Wilson Center Library. Last, but certainly not least, I wish to thank Mary Lenn Dixon, editor-in-chief of Texas A&M University Press, and Diana L. Vance, editorial assistant for acquisitions at the press, for their unflagging interest in this project and their hard work, and also the two anonymous readers for their helpful feedback.

THE LIBERAL PROJECT
AND THE TRANSFORMATION
OF DEMOCRACY

1

INTRODUCTION

This book figures as a defense of liberalism, but not in the sense in which it is commonly understood. What has come to be understood and championed under the rubric of *liberalism* is often very different from what it was at the time it was developed. In defending liberalism, then, I am returning to the classics, in order to provide a basis for analyzing what has been happening in Eastern Europe (and, by extension, in the world more broadly) and to chart an alternative future for liberalism.[1] In this spirit, I have undertaken to extend the argument first broached in my 1997 publication *Whose Democracy?* to the effect that moral relativism, nationalism (in the sense in which I define it), and capitalism all present challenges to the project of establishing, consolidating, and maintaining legitimate (and hence, stable) political systems, and to the effect that the standard for system legitimacy is Natural Law or, as I called it in my earlier work, Universal Reason.[2]

Recently, there have been claims registered on behalf of certain notions about cultural diversity to the effect that there are no universal standards, no universal rights, and, above all, no such thing as Universal Reason, which is to say, no universally valid mores of human behavior. Moral relativists choosing to take up this particular banner may be overstating their case. "After all," Shashi Tharoor reminds us, "concepts of justice and law, the legitimacy of government, the dignity of the individual, protection from oppressive or arbitrary rule, and participation in the affairs of the community are found in every society on the face of the earth. Far from being difficult to identify, the number of philosophical common denominators between different cultures and political traditions makes universalism anything but a distortion of reality."[3]

The words "found in every society" establish the universalism of certain minimal truths; there is no need to insist on universal assent in order to establish the universality of a minimal moral law, any more than one would need to insist on universal assent to the laws of mathematics in order to establish that the laws of physics have a legitimate claim to universal and transcultural validity. In order to insist on the nullibicity of universal standards of behavior, a would-be consistent relativist would have to maintain that murder, torture, the killing of infants, mass rape, pickpocketing, lying, slavery, cruelty, insulting one's hosts, and other forms of hurtful behavior are not necessarily wrong or even morally problematic. In order to connect this with *misconceived* notions of cultural diversity, he or she would have to claim further that at least one of these behaviors is or could be considered a local tradition in some country or other. That said, it should be clear enough why I consider such relativists to be either unconscious of the import of their own words or, alternatively, driven by contempt for non-Europeans; the typical charge against classical liberal notions of universal rights and mores that they are Eurocentric is, in practice, not so much a charge as a claim.

Yet, far from being mere Eurocentric conceits, as the cultural relativists suppose, honesty, generosity, hospitality, kindness, loyalty, and mutual aid have been found by anthropologists to be universally held to be important virtues in societies at all levels of development, on all continents.[4] No one (as far as I am aware) denies that there are variations in customs, traditions, and even mores from one society to another, from one group (however defined) to another. What Natural Law theorists insist, however, is that not everything is arbitrary or relative or merely a feature of one or another religion or culture.

Natural Law has also encountered resistance among authoritarians of various stripes, because they are aware that it establishes the concept of an external standard by which the conduct of state authorities may be judged. As Heinrich Rommen put it in a 1945 publication, "There must be a law from which all human laws derive their validity and moral obligation. There must be a right which is paramount to all rights of the state."[5]

The Natural Law tradition constitutes the single most important area of overlap between Catholic social teachings and the classical liberal tradition of John Locke, Thomas Jefferson, James Madison, and Immanuel Kant.[6] And, in spite of recurrent announcements from time to time that Natural Law theory is "dead" or—worse for some—"old-fashioned," Natural Law continues to animate scholars and, in the past hundred years, has penetrated deeply into international law. The Geneva Convention and the Universal Declaration of Human Rights are but two of the better known incarnations in international law of the Natural Law tradition. What is Natural Law? In a word, it is the set of moral precepts that are embedded in human reason and can be understood as binding without recourse to divine law, ecclesiastical precepts, or the laws of the state. These precepts have universal validity, applying to all equally, and the basic postulates of the moral law can be discerned by unaided reason (by all, with the possible exceptions of psychopaths and sociopaths). There are some variations on the theme, of course. St. Thomas Aquinas argued that, beyond the "basic postulates," unaided reason might well run into difficulty; hence, for Aquinas, the need for divine revelation.[7] For Richard Hooker and Locke, the most central postulates discernible by reason are the imperative to do no harm and the moral equality of all persons.[8] For Thomas Hobbes, by contrast with Aquinas, Hooker, and Locke alike, Natural Law cannot be authoritatively interpreted by common folk and stands in need of definitive interpretation by the sovereign.[9] For Kant, the door opened by reason is the categorical imperative, the rule of universalizability which, for Kant, is the fulcrum of the moral law.

Postmodernists are variously embarrassed, annoyed, repulsed, or bored by appeals to Natural Law. But, to my mind, Universal Reason (Natural Law) is the standard whereby to measure not just human behavior but also system legitimacy; and system legitimacy—understood triadically as the degree to which a state's citizens judge the system to be in conformity with moral standards, its own political rules (laws), and notions of economic equity—is the barometer of a system's stability, providing at the same time the key to understanding both its internal and its external behavior.

Moral universalism is the term appropriately applied to adherents of the Natural Law tradition. It may be distinguished in the first place from *moral consequentialism,* which seeks to assess the morality of an action not according to abstract principles (as both Locke and Kant would have it) but according to the actual or presumed consequences of the action. John Stuart Mill was this school's greatest champion. *Moral conventionalism,* another historic rival, consists in the denial that there can exist any authoritative standards or rule of behavior other than those laid down in law, and hence also no external standard against which to measure the justice of the laws. Thrasymachus, the Sophist mocked in Book I of Plato's *Republic,* is the earliest known advocate of moral conventionalism. Hobbes, too, takes a conventionalist position, asking, rhetorically, in *On the Citizen,* "How many Rebellions have been caused by the doctrine that it is up to private men to determine whether the commands of Kings are just or unjust, and that his commands may rightly be discussed before they are carried out?"[10]

Other moral understandings include *moral contractarianism* (according to which morality consists in unwritten and largely implicit rules of behavior passed down from generation to generation, but, for the most part, not open to rational review or legislative correction), and *theocracy* (according to which society should be modeled according to the precepts of divine law, as interpreted by the clergy of the self-declared "true religion"). Aside from these moral understandings, there is also the position of *nihilism,* which rejects all mores, codes, rules, commandments, and institutions as arrant nonsense. The only strict nihilist with whose work I am familiar is Max Stirner, author of *The Ego and His Own* (1844), a book aptly described as an assemblage of meandering ravings.[11] To this list one may perhaps add *pure relativism,* using the word "pure" to distinguish this position from the alternative positions that morality is relative either to the law or to the word of God properly interpreted or to traditions; by contrast with these traditions, which still assert some point of reference outside the individual, pure relativism is the view that, not only is each individual person entitled to reach his or her own judgments about morality, but each individual is also entitled to establish his or her own criteria and standards for morality, even if it is nothing grander than "I feel like it," or she may offer no criteria or standards at all. This position is uniquely postmodern and will either expire of its own vapidity or contribute to the ruination of any sense of community.

I have insisted on identifying myself with the Natural Law tradition rather than with "liberalism-in-general," even though I consider myself a classical liberal, for three reasons: first, because my ideas about economic legitimacy (viz., that neither socialism nor capitalism is legitimate) derive, in the first place, from the encyclicals of Popes Leo XIII, John XXIII, and John Paul II, encyclicals that take Natural Law as their point of departure; second, because among the three strands of liberalism that have emerged— universalism-idealism (embodying Natural Law), conventionalism-realism, and consequentialism—I identify myself with the first, universalism-idealism; and third, because the term *Natural Law* is far more precise than *liberalism,* which, in any event, is all too frequently identified with the specific cultural dispositions, laws, customs, strengths, weaknesses, and proclivities of American society, even though not everything occurring in America should be interpreted as a pristine embodiment of classical liberal principles.[12]

The twin themes of Natural Law and liberal idealism run as threads through the entire text. In chapter 2, I develop a theory about classical liberalism, outlining at greater length than I have done here the sundry strands of liberalism. There I outline the central principles of classical liberalism and the central operative principles of democracy, allowing one to view liberal democracy as a compound of liberalism, understood as a moral framework, and democracy, understood as a political formula. In chapter 3, I consider the challenges capitalism has offered to the liberal project in Eastern Europe, noting, along the way, the insights of various scholars who anticipated the region's rough ride in the immediate postcommunist era. It would be comforting to imagine that capitalism unbound—even, ideally, where out-and-out mafias are concerned—would somehow work, as if by an invisible hand (to steal a phrase from Adam Smith) to foster the common good. But if by capitalism we mean a system premised on minimal government regulation, geared to the maximization of profits, and oriented toward inculcating in consumers cravings for the commodities offered for purchase, then capitalism may, in fact, be problematic for the liberal project (to put it gently). Capitalism, as Joseph Schumpeter put it once, "creates a critical frame of mind which, after having destroyed the moral authority of so many other institutions, in the end turns against its own; the bourgeois finds to his amazement that the rationalist attitude does not stop at the credentials of kings and popes but goes on to attack private property and the whole scheme of bourgeois values."[13]

In chapter 4, I take up the concept of sovereignty, examining its development by Thomas Hobbes, Jean-Jacques Rousseau, and Immanuel Kant and inquiring as to how the constitutions of the contemporary East European states may reflect perspectives expostulated in these theories about sovereignty. Chapter 5 picks up where chapter 3 leaves off, probing the alleged right of national self-determination and subjecting it to a moral critique. The idea of a right of national self-determination is, further, shown to be organically connected with the tradition of realism (which is to say, with the rejection of Natural Law, even though Natural Law is the only foundation upon which claims on behalf of natural rights may be coherently registered), and with certain misconceived efforts to introduce exaggerated and distorted notions about value-free science into the social sciences and

humanities. From the analysis in chapters 3 and 4 it follows that neither
ethnic homogeneity nor nationalist ideology has anything to do with the
Natural Law tradition or, if one prefers, with liberal idealism. Quite to
the contrary, whereas liberal idealism enumerates certain principles that are
essential to the establishment and maintenance of a legitimate system,
nationalism pulls one in precisely the opposite direction, toward illegitimate politics. Whereas liberal idealism holds that the state should be seen
as a rational construct, designed to foster the common good and obliged to
respect the limits set by Natural Law, "nationalism and racialism regard
the state as the fruit from the mysterious depth of an irrational, national
soul. . . . [The] State, consequently, is not the creation of reason for reason,"
and cannot be limited by the dictates of Universal Reason, but is merely,
for nationalists, the sword and shield of the ruling nation.[14] The nationalist
principle obtained one of its earliest defenses in the writings of the Abbé
E. J. Sièyes, one of five members of the French Revolutionary Directory.
It was he who advised that "[the Nation's] will is always lawful, for she is
herself the embodiment of the law."[15]

Then, in chapter 6, I outline three models of church–state condominium as they have been embodied in contemporary Central Europe:
clerical democracy, illustrated by the case of Poland; the laic state, illustrated by the case of the Czech Republic; and an unstable hybrid of these
two principles, illustrated by the case of Slovakia. From the Polish case, it
emerges that, in spite of the vital contribution to Natural Law theory made,
in the first place, by Aquinas but also by the three popes whose encyclicals
I have mentioned above, in practice the Church has taken positions that
may be criticized from the standpoint of Natural Law.

Chapter 7 extends the analysis to the situation of women in Eastern
Europe, noting the various ways women in the region have suffered differentially since 1989. In this context, I suggest that classical liberalism, designed to address the concerns and issues of the eighteenth century, must
be extended along lines that strengthen the commitment to the central principles of liberalism, and I urge that liberalism acknowledge that the equality of women is intrinsic to the liberal project, acknowledge that animals
and even species have rights (pointing to a right of a species to survive), and
make protection of the environment a priority.

In chapter 8, I ask the big question, What is the purpose of political
association? Stating an answer provides a basis for assessing the extent to
which liberalism and/or democracy may serve to realize that perceived pur-

pose or set of purposes. In the same chapter, I look at permutations of democracy and consider their vulnerabilities to corruption. Finally, in the closing chapter, I summarize the chief arguments of the book, returning to the theme of legitimacy and noting that the high value placed upon it by liberal idealists distinguishes them from liberal realists.

2

LIBERALISM AND THE MORAL LAW, THEN AND NOW

Some forty years ago, when I was a senior in high school, I took a class popularly called "Senior Problems." The class was, in fact, an introduction to philosophy and it was there that I first encountered the pre-Socratic philosophers, and, in particular, Heraclitus, the great philosopher of change. Heraclitus is famous for having said that one cannot step into the same river twice and he emphasized that everything is always changing. As anyone who has ever read the fragments which remain of the pre-Socratics (actually quotations and paraphrases of their ideas embodied in the works of later writers) will remember, Heraclitus's nemesis was Parmenides, who liked to say that change was an illusion and that things remained basically the same. I suspect that the difference between Heraclitus and Parmenides was not one of substance so much as one of focus, or, if one prefers, of emphasis. Be that as it may, Heraclitus's lesson that everything changes is a good place to begin our discussion of liberalism—not because anyone would think of Heraclitus as a liberal (I certainly do not make that claim) but rather because liberalism too changes, evolves, shifts emphasis, finds new supporters and new enemies, and tackles new challenges.

If one thinks of liberalism as a doctrine of individual rights—perhaps the simplest way to express what is often taken to be the central feature of the liberal tradition—one immediately confronts two important facts: first, the notion that individuals have rights may be traced back to Hammurabi's

code ("an eye for an eye"—a right to retribution) in the eighteenth century
B.C.E. and, indeed, even farther back than that; and second, that, as L. W.
Sumner has noted (among many others),[1] every notion of rights presumes
and entails a notion of duties. In other words, a doctrine of individual rights
is, at the same time, a doctrine of individual duties and, if the individual
is granted rights against the state, also a doctrine of the duties of the state.
Indeed, notions of rights and duties may be found throughout the ancient
world. In ancient Egypt, such acts as murder, theft, adultery, lying, ignoring
the truth, eavesdropping, and speaking without thinking were considered
acts against the Goddess Ma'at, who was the protector of truth, order,
and cosmic balance.[2] Similarly, in ancient Sumer, children were raised to
respect "truth, the art of being forthright" and "the art of kindness," among
other virtues to be cultivated (with Plato giving the classic expression of this
position).[3] The ancients considered moral law to be intrinsic, i.e., not dependent on written or statutory law. In fact, there are three facets of liberalism—the rule of law, respect for the harm principle, and an appeal to the
moral law—which turn out to have enjoyed transhistorical recognition, being accepted in almost all societies since the dawn of civilization.

But the earliest appeal to natural reason or right reason—which
would become a hallmark of the liberal Enlightenment—may be found in
the writings of the Roman philosopher and politician Marcus Tullius Cicero
(106–43 B.C.E.), who argued that right reason was a sure guide to moral action and advised his readers to let reason rule their passions. Later, in the
13th century, Thomas Aquinas (1224–1274), a Dominican priest and teacher
of theology, wrote his *Summa Theologica,* arguing that Natural Reason consists of both primary principles, which never change (such as the injunc-
tion to choose good over evil), and secondary principles, which reflect at
most the level of wisdom of the age or local practices and which, accordingly, may change. Natural Reason or Natural Law was generally acknowledged throughout Western Christendom in the Middle Ages and, indeed,
until the eighteenth century. Neither Cicero nor Aquinas was a liberal by
any stretch of the imagination, but they formed part of the heritage on
which the liberals would later build. I dare say that, without their contributions, classical liberalism might have taken a different path.

THE BRITISH ENLIGHTENMENT, 1593–1704

I am demarcating the period under discussion from the publication of
Books I–IV of Richard Hooker's *Of the Laws of Ecclesiastical Polity* to the
death of John Locke. While this period represents the incunabulum of

the liberal tradition, the liberal tradition has continued to evolve in a series of waves. Richard Hooker (1554–1600), chief pastor of one of the more important centers of legal learning in London, may be counted as a "pre-liberal," both because of the content of his writings and because of his influence on John Locke (1632–1704). Hooker articulated a clear postulate: Bearing in mind that one does not want to be harmed oneself, one should not harm anyone else. This has come down in classical liberalism as "the harm principle." Hooker also took over the concept of Natural Law, writing that

> . . . by the force of the light of reason, wherewith God illuminateth everyone which cometh into the world, men being enabled to know truth from falsehood, and good from evil, do thereby learn in many things what the will of God is. . . . The main principles of reason are in themselves apparent. For to make nothing evident of itself until man's understanding were to take away all possibility of knowing anything.[4]

Locke, whose *Second Treatise on Government* is replete with references to "the Judicious Hooker," took the existence of Natural Law as a given and described its central principle as "that being all equal and independent, no one ought to harm another in his Life, Health, Liberty or Possessions."[5] Both in *Two Treatises* and in *Letters on Toleration* Locke declared that people had natural rights which no government had the authority to abridge, and that, in the religious sphere, members of minority groups had the right to toleration. Locke also postulated a basic equality among people. Thus, by the time we reach Locke, we have a clear articulation of individual rights, tolerance, respect for the harm principle, human equality (at least among males), and religious tolerance. Add to this the principle of the rule of law, which Locke, like other liberals, presumed and which, in any case, has been an accepted principle of legitimacy in all states since the dawn of civilization (whether honored or not), and we have the *classical liberal project* in full bloom.

Locke conjoined these principles to a vigorous defense of private property. Writing at a time when the enclosure movement was dividing British society, Locke took the position that enclosing land for agricultural use did no harm to those whose livelihood depended on the grazing of animals, as long as there was enough land left which had not been enclosed. We shall return to this point later. For now, I shall be content to note that Locke's linkage of property with individual right was also taken over by the Scottish philosopher David Hume and the German philosopher Immanuel Kant (1724–1804) and directly influenced the thinking of Thomas Jefferson and James Madison in their drafting of the founding documents of the United States.[6]

Thomas Hobbes (1588–1679), the author of *Leviathan* and *De Cive,* was most definitely *not* part of the British Enlightenment; on the contrary, with his exhortation to set up in power anyone capable of maintaining order and with his declaration that it was up to the sovereign to interpret the Natural Law for all his citizens,[7] thereby nullifying the sovereignty of reason,[8] he set himself pointedly against the spirit of Enlightenment and on the side of reaction. He would become part of the liberal story only in the twentieth century, as will be noted below.

LIBERALISM IN THE EIGHTEENTH CENTURY: A FLOWERING OF UNIVERSALISM

Where the eighteenth century is concerned, one may speak of three giants of liberalism: Immanuel Kant, Tom Paine (1737–1809), and Mary Wollstonecraft (1759–1797)—listed here in the order of their births. To this list one may add Jean-Jacques Rousseau (1712–1778), author of *The Social Contract,* although his advocacy of state-controlled, state-sponsored religion makes for an ill fit with mainstream liberalism. Each of these figures brought something new to liberalism, and urged upon it new tasks and challenges.

Where Locke and his employer, Anthony Ashley Cooper, the Earl of Shaftesbury, had worked to weaken the Crown and to build up the power of parliament, which is to say, the power of the middle classes,[9] Rousseau and Paine dedicated themselves to working for the good of the working classes, the latter even being elected to the French National Assembly, in spite of his ignorance of French. Tom Paine famously sketched out an elaborate pension plan to be financed by progressive taxation, so that no one should have to live out his life in indigent conditions. Insofar as Rousseau's ideas paved the way for and contributed to the ideology of the French Revolution and insofar as Paine sat in the revolutionary assembly, both may be identified at least in part with that revolution. Neither Rousseau nor Paine had a lasting influence on the liberal tradition, however, in spite of their originality and personal courage. In Rousseau's case, this was largely because his thought gave rise to a large number of mutually exclusive interpretations,[10] so that, even today, there is no consensus as to what Rousseau intended with his writings. As for Paine, his proposals were radical even by the radical standards of his day, and with the publication of his anti-religious *Age of Reason,* he assured the lasting enmity of many of his contemporaries. The lasting importance of Paine's work, however, is to demonstrate that liberal notions could be separated from the Christian framework in which Locke had embedded them and to show that within liberalism there was the possibility for advocacy of strong state intervention on behalf of the working class and the poor. The lasting importance of Rousseau's work is to have forced people to think about the dangers in following blindly the general will of the people, even if Rousseau himself expressed optimism that the general will would always turn out for the best.

Immanuel Kant, like the ancients and like his liberal antecedents, was convinced that the moral law was intrinsic, which is to say that there are things which are intrinsically right, and things which are intrinsically wrong. His sketch of the categorical imperative—"Act upon a maxim that can also hold as a universal law"[11]—was intended, not to reduce morality to pure subjectivity, but, on the contrary, to provide a guide for determining which actions are in accord with the moral law, and which contrary. For Kant, it was the actor's intention that was determinative of the moral content of the action, and he specifically rejected any appeal to consequences as irrelevant to assessing the morality of an action. Kant made several major contributions to the liberal tradition. First, he reaffirmed the centrality of morality in politics; second, he separated liberalism from democracy, by arguing that a government may be "republican" in content, but monarchical in form; third, he argued that the project "of establishing a perfect civil constitution is subordinate to the problem of a law-governed external relationship with other states, and cannot be solved unless the latter is also solved";[12] and fourth, he offered an articulate defense of idealism, which I have defined elsewhere as "the belief that sovereignty is relative to morality and that governments should be held to a universal moral standard."[13] Kant also took note of animal rights, arguing that animals have rights, but no demonstrable duties.[14]

Mary Wollstonecraft, a noted writer, is best known for her books, *A Vindication of the Rights of Men* (1790) and *A Vindication of the Rights of Woman* (1791). Wollstonecraft's great contribution was to show that the liberal project, with its insistence on equality and on respect for the harm principle, could only be judged to be seriously flawed as long as women were treated as inferior to men whether in social, economic, political, or other terms. Stressing the importance of education in shaping people's views, she was also a foe of monarchical rule, standing armies, and pre-arranged marriages, and a defender of animals against maltreatment.

Kant, Paine, Wollstonecraft, and even Rousseau presumed the existence of a universally valid moral code, which reason could access, at least in part. They were all, thus, moral universalists. But Paine and Wollstonecraft, in particular, broadened and extended the liberal project by demanding that its principles be explicitly extended to embrace the working class and women, while Kant provided the most comprehensive and systematic moral system since Plato.

LIBERALISM IN THE NINETEENTH CENTURY: THE CONSEQUENTIALIST CHALLENGE

Consequentialism—the doctrine that the moral content of actions should be judged not according to some presumably universal precepts or according to the intentions of the actors, but by their consequences—owes its origin to the British utilitarians: Jeremy Bentham, James Mill, and his son, John Stuart Mill. Bentham and the younger Mill both rejected Kant's premises—Mill respectfully,[15] Bentham rather more brusquely. For Bentham, "there are no such things as natural rights [and hence, no such thing as Natural Law]—no such things as rights anterior to the establishment of government [as Locke had urged]—no such things as natural rights opposed to, in contradistinction to, legal [rights] . . . *Natural rights* is simple nonsense: natural and imprescriptible rights, rhetorical nonsense—nonsense upon stilts."[16]

The heart of the consequentialists' challenge to universalism was the dual assertion that conscience may be a guide to the purity of the actor's motive but provides no clue as to the morality of the action as such and that what is moral is what is good for people (and, by extension, other living beings). For the consequentialists, it makes no sense to speak of an action being good if it is not good for anybody. But the question as to what is good is a complex one which the younger Mill explored in his *Utilitarianism* (1861). Here he stressed that higher pleasures should be preferred over lower pleasures and that, in the event of a conflict, it would be best not to sacrifice a higher pleasure for the sake of obtaining a lower one.

Mill's greatest works—*On Liberty* (1859), *Utilitarianism* (1861), *Considerations on Representative Government* (1861), and *The Subjection of Women* (1869) were all written within a decade of the death of his marriage partner and lifelong friend Harriet Taylor (in 1858), whom he credits for having collaborated in generating some of the ideas in these works. *On Liberty* is best remembered for its assertion that even if the entire planet save for one person were of one opinion and only one person holding to a contrary view, that person had every right to his opinion. Mill makes clear his motivation here, claiming that all human progress comes through the challenging of accepted paradigms and ways of thought and that the pioneers of progress are always the rebels. Thus, for him, the freedom of all is important above all because it assures the freedom for geniuses to work. This same orientation is also reflected in his *Considerations,* where he warns against various dangers that can debase democracy, but expresses optimism that as long as there is a core of educated and noble characters in the government, representative government has a chance of functioning at its best. In this work, he also emphasizes that a free debate is the best assurance of reasoned policy.

Inevitably, Mill's radical ideas about freedom of opinion would also carry over into his views of tolerance. Specifically, where Locke had championed the principle of tolerance in the religious sphere, Mill extended that principle to other spheres, being limited only by the harm principle.[17] This principle, that one should never willfully do harm to another, except in defense of some valued person or object, lies at the heart of the consequentialist position and receives explicit formulation in *Utilitarianism,* where Mill writes,

> The moral rules which forbid mankind to hurt one another (in which one must never forget to include wrongful interference with each other's freedom) are more vital to human well-being than any maxims, however important, which only point out the best mode of managing some department of human affairs.[18]

Mill served one term in Parliament (1865–68) and is on record as having been the first MP to urge that women be granted the right to vote in Great Britain. Mill's influence among liberals was huge and for more than a century after the completion of the major works mentioned above, he was considered the father of modern liberalism.[19] It was only in the 1970s that his star began to fade, among other things as a result of the neo-Kantian revival.

LIBERALISM IN THE TWENTIETH CENTURY: THE RETURN OF HOBBES AND THE RISE OF CONVENTIONALISM

In his own day, Thomas Hobbes had been treated as a kind of Satan. There were several reasons for this, among them his reductionist attitude toward Christian religion and his grant that the sovereign could determine the content of Natural Law for all of his citizens. At that time, it would not have occurred to anyone to describe Hobbes as a liberal. But even in the eighteenth century, Hobbes exerted some influence on the thinking of such American liberals as Thomas Jefferson and James Madison, and, more recently, Hobbes enjoyed a revival in the twentieth century, with repeated scholarly efforts to represent Locke (inaccurately) as replying in his *Two Treatises* to Hobbes, rather than to Sir Robert Filmer, contributing to an increasing tendency to allow that Hobbes, while no liberal, has something to do with the pre-history of liberalism.

Perhaps he does. But what interests me in this context is that the revival of interest in Hobbes was also associated with two other trends: the rise of so-called realism in international politics and the appearance of a conventionalist current within the liberal tradition. By conventionalism I mean the notion that what is moral and immoral is not a factor of Natural Law or Universal Reason, and not a factor of the greatest good for the greatest number, but is, rather, a factor of what the law says it is. For pure conventionalists, to put it in a word, morality is not intrinsic, but extrinsic. And thus, rape, for example, is wrong because people have agreed that it is wrong and have codified their consensus in law. The absence of a law signifies an absence of consensus, which in turn means that the moral content of an action has not been determined for the given community.

From my own point of view, it seems to me that the three greatest liberal thinkers of the twentieth century—measuring greatness by originality of contribution, prominence, and influence—were Hannah Arendt (1906–1975), John Rawls (1921–2002), and Jürgen Habermas (1929–). Arendt's writings were, at least in part, stimulated by her personal outrage at the horrors of Nazi extermination camps in World War II and in her work on totalitarianism, she offered a biting criticism of anti-Semitism, totalitarianism, and imperialism alike, viewing the last of the three as a necessary consequence of the first two.[20]

Rawls' great contributions included a passionate defense of Kant's moral philosophy and his own theory of Justice as Fairness, which he defined as consisting

> of two principles: that all have the greatest degree of liberty compatible with like liberty for all, and that social and economic inequalities be attached to positions open to all under fair equality of opportunity and to the greatest benefit of the least well-off members of society. The first of these two principles is known as the liberty principle, while

the second half of the second, reflecting the idea that inequality is only justified if to the advantage of those who are less well-off, is known as the difference principle.[21]

Rawls is also known for his use of a fictive "original position," which he defined as a situation of bargaining in which people should design the world in which they wished to live without knowing whether they would be male or female, healthy or strong, a member of a locally dominant race or a local minority race, rich or poor. He argued that, in such a situation, any sane person would seek to protect the weak and the sick, and that, therefore, this provided a reasonable standard to which societies should aspire.

Rawls in fact used the term *reasonable,* rather than *rational,* because of the former's more modest claims. He also preached a pluralism of political ideas. As he wrote in *Political Liberalism,* "Holding a political conception as true, and for that reason alone the one suitable basis of public reason, is exclusive, even sectarian, and so likely to foster political division."[22] This is also a clue to Rawls' originality: Rawls was neither a universalist nor a conventionalist, but rather occupied the point where the two traditions came together. He viewed public morality as reflecting the consensus of reasonable minds aspiring to a reasonable solution. This is light-years away from Hobbes' iron-fisted sovereign, who was empowered to dictate what was right and wrong, but it is also distinct from Kant's conviction that there are some truths which are objective and which can be discerned by reason.

Finally, in the twentieth century (and into the twenty-first) there is the towering figure of Jürgen Habermas, long-time professor of philosophy at the University of Frankfurt and the author of some two dozen books. In *The Inclusion of the Other,*[23] for example, Habermas revives the Kantian project of organizing the international community on the basis of public reason and offers that project as a suitable basis for reducing the incidence of regional conflicts. Habermas is, in fact, the most influential Kantian alive today. What Arendt, Rawls, and Habermas have added to the liberal project may be summed by the triad *compassion, justice as fairness,* and *a plea for public reason.*

But while these refinements were being made in the academy, conventional understandings of liberalism and of rights were also evolving, and not in parallel. Specifically, at the dawn of the twentieth century, in both Europe and the United States, there was a broad consensus that individual rights could and should be limited when the needs of the community so dictated. This was poignantly illustrated in the debate around and eventual passage of the sterilization act in Indiana in 1907, which showed that the majority of Indianans were utterly convinced of the right of the state to authorize the involuntary sterilization of those who were deemed "defective." Indeed, so widespread was this attitude in the early twentieth century that similar laws were passed at the state level throughout the United States as well as in various European countries, including Germany and Norway.[24] There were also assumptions and attitudes connected with social class, which entailed relations of deference and subordination.

Three things contributed to changing all of this. The first was the two world wars, which destroyed the three major traditional monarchical systems of Europe and accelerated the process of erosion in relations of deference and subordination. The second was the sexual revolution of the 1960s, which largely destroyed the traditional attitude that sexual relations should be reserved for one's life-partner and should be considered the highest expression of love and loyalty, replacing that with the attitude that sexual relations are about physical self-gratification and that every individual has a "right" to have as much sex as he or she wants, at least prior to marriage. The sexual revolution also had a legal component, as shown in the case of *Griswold v. Connecticut,* in which birth control was found to be not inconsistent with the U.S. Constitution. The case also provided the occasion for the Supreme Court's recognition of a constitutional right to privacy, which, also inspired by sexual relations, was extended to other spheres as well.[25] The third factor was the commercialization of popular culture beginning in the 1970s and the largely successful promotion of materialism— commodities—as the highest measure of personal achievement and happiness. This last factor resulted in a debasing of concepts of rights and freedom, which have come to be commonly understood as "my right to buy a new VCR" or "my freedom to play my new stereo as loudly as I wish." As a recent American television ad puts it, "Reclaim your manhood—buy a Hummer." While Kant considered that one's rights were limited to the right to behave morally and insisted that there was no right to behave in an evil way, it is easy to find people today who argue that, on the contrary, the heart of freedom lies precisely in the freedom to do evil. This attitude is reflected in the proliferation of cursing among many members of the younger generation as well as in more serious acts. Notice too that a claim to enjoy a freedom to do as one pleases entails also a rejection of the harm principle. And when one considers that what passes for tolerance today is often no more than apathy and that the most organized special interest group in the United States, the Christian Right, has been actively campaigning to insinuate its doctrines into public law,[26] the conclusion is unavoidable that everyday "liberalism," at least in the United States, is a very cheap alloy of the original classical liberalism. Where Locke and Kant preached the rule of law, individual rights, tolerance, respect for the harm principle, equality, and neutrality of the state in matters of religion, in everyday parlance not one of these, not even the rule of law, remains unscathed.

THE CHALLENGES AHEAD

But all is not lost. To highlight problems is not to say that the entire society is plagued by these problems. And it is precisely among those sectors unaffected by the cult of materialism and the conceit of omniscience that one can find reasons for hope.

At the present point in time, there are several interlocking challenges that threaten the survival of humankind and of most life on this planet. These challenges are global warming (first recognized in the early 1970s but largely ignored until very recently), the destruction of habitats and accompanying extinction of species, world overpopulation and the incipient strain on world food supplies, the melting of the polar ice caps, which threatens to flood many densely inhabited areas, and, perhaps ironically, an increasing shortage of potable water. If human rights include a right to survive, then, even at the crudest level, these challenges become challenges for liberals.

Moreover, there is a growing contingent of writers who argue variously that species have a right to survive and that animals have rights (a point made earlier by Kant, it will be recalled). There have even been questions raised as to whether trees enjoy some moral standing. Moreover, even though animals (and trees) are not in a position to assert their rights in a court of law, it would be possible to authorize an agency or organization to advocate the rights of animals and represent them in court.[27] This entails abandoning the notion that animals are property and recognizing them as *persons* who, like children, may have guardians, but not owners.[28] Thus, the destruction of habitats and the damage done by global warming and its various side effects do not only violate human rights; they also violate animal rights. Earlier, I referred to Locke's defense of the enclosure movement, but, as I noted there, his defense was based on the presumption of sufficiency of grazing land for the grazers. Applying that principle of sufficiency to today, one could say that environmental protectionism was at least implicitly anticipated in Locke's classic statement.

The old formula of classical liberalism is still, in my view, a noble project, an appropriate formula for a legitimate state, and the only reasonable basis for any moral-legal system. But liberalism has been evolving and expanding in new directions throughout history, as I have tried to demonstrate with this brief historical overview, and classical liberalism, however noble, must be extended and expanded if it is to meet the challenges we already face.

3

LIBERALISM AND CAPITALISM
An Unhappy Marriage

ore than a decade and a half ago, as Eastern Europe began a process of transformation of its political, economic, moral, and cultural systems, many there allowed themselves to feel jubilant (though not in Yugoslavia, where tensions were already running high and fear was the dominant emotion). Berliners danced on the Wall that had divided their city for a generation and pocketed pieces of it as the bull-dozers knocked down the most striking symbol of East–West division. In much of the region, especially in the northern tier, there were widespread demands for privatization, property restitution, and an end to constraints on free enterprise. In Western governments, there was smug satisfaction. U.S. President George Bush even announced the dawning of a "New World Or-der," no doubt oblivious to the fact that just sixty years earlier the Third Reich and its allies had been promoting what they called the "New Order."

But not everyone was smug. Among scholars, caution was more com-mon than delirium. Economist Laura D'Andrea Tyson, for example, in an in-sightful article published in 1991, pointed out that "although continued change is a certainty, its ultimate destination is not. No one knows precisely where reforms will lead. The only certainties are that the road of change will be a rocky one and that economic performance will very likely get worse be-fore it gets better." Predicting "a sharp decline" in available government rev-enues, leading to cuts in "all categories of domestic spending—investment, consumption, and government spending," she forecast years of "austerity,"

"popular discontent," and "dislocation." Rejecting triumphalism and deter-
minism alike, she concluded soberly that "the challenges of transition are
monumental and complicated ones. The process of addressing these challenges will be long and arduous. Not all countries will succeed, and their
final destination points will be different." [1]

About the same time, Ivo Banac predicted that "the dislocations en-
demic to systemic changes will keep Eastern Europe boiling for years,"
while Katherine Verdery and Gail Kligman observed accurately that "the situation in Romania is more complex than may appear." Again, writing of the
case of Albania, Elež Biberaj observed that "the transition from centrally
planned communism to market-driven capitalism will be a complicated process" and noted that "some observers have warned of the danger of a conservative communist backlash and authoritarian regression." [2]

András Kepes, in a contribution written for the same volume in which
Tyson's piece appeared, expressed his fear that, due to the weakness of the
fledgling multiparty system in Hungary, "the demand of the masses for authoritarianism may gain ground," noting that the sharp increase in the crime
rate represented an important challenge to the postcommunist system. [3]
Meanwhile, Kenneth Jowitt confidently predicted that "Klaus's economic
reforms [in the Czech Republic] will fail" and, responding to sundry complications across the region, suggested that an alternative path of "liberal authoritarianism" might constitute a more practical strategy. [4]

Nor were they alone in their caution. Patricia Smith, commenting on
the East German case in 1991, concluded that "the quick route to the market economy has [already] proven to be more costly, difficult, and painful
than originally anticipated," [5] while the ever-observant Anneli Ute Gabanyi
was quick to point out the difficulties in Romania's convoluted transition. [6]
Or again, Enikő Bollobás, writing in November 1991, expressed concern that
"the problem of ultra-nationalism will get more and more complicated and
more difficult to solve." [7] Similarly, György Tokay and Dorin Tudoran, writing
in April 1992, stressed that "the gap between talking about democratic values and behaving in such a manner is enormous." [8]

Some of the challenges facing the region at the dawn of the postcommunist era were clear enough. As I wrote in 1991:

> Institutions can be closed or created, laws can be rewritten. But atti-
> tudes and behaviors are sometimes harder to change. . . . Taken col-
> lectively, this [postcommunist] attitudinal syndrome . . . gives one rea-
> son for pause. [Some of] these attitudes are clearly not supportive of

pluralism. . . . [This] suggest[s] that alongside the very real factors for (re)pluralization, there are also some factors that will pull in the opposite direction. Political change will not be easy.[9]

Democracy has conditions and preconditions, and unless the key conditions are fulfilled—such as the rule of law, a free press, an independent judiciary, and multicandidate elections, with the system largely free of corruption and plutocratic influence—system building may fall short of expectations; and hence too, "the stability of any democratic system cannot be taken for granted."[10]

Yet, if many observers forecast a difficult transition, none, as far as I am aware, was so bold as to suggest that the aspirations of these societies would necessarily meet with complete and total defeat, much less that these societies were doomed to an eternity of economic instability, widespread crime and corruption, and regional turmoil. Robert Kaplan's mass market "travelogue," *Balkan Ghosts,* came perhaps the closest to complete pessimism, though only about the Balkans, and even Kaplan would later deny that he had intended his book to be interpreted as offering either analysis or prognosis.

Where Yugoslavia is concerned, Ivo Banac and Viktor Meier offered realistic and insightful analyses of the situation, long before war broke out. Already in November 1990, Banac warned that Serbian party boss Slobodan Milošević was taking the country down the road to civil war,[11] while Meier's regular reports for the *Frankfurter Allgemeine* provided a clear day-by-day, week-by-week chronicle of Yugoslavia's descent into interethnic violence.[12]

While Serbia, Croatia, and Bosnia-Herzegovina went to war, other countries in the region looked for foreign investors to bail them out of their economic doldrums, in effect selling their stock to the highest bidder. In summer 1991, for instance, Kazimierz Poznański warned that the penetration of the region by foreign investors risked creating relations of dependence of the region on private stockholders in the West.[13] The advantage of such dependence was that it offered the prospect of keeping the economy functioning, while creating or maintaining a certain number of jobs. The drawbacks were twofold: first, by selling their stock to foreign owners, the East Europeans inevitably gave up some of the control they might otherwise—in an "ideal" world—have enjoyed over their own future and, in the process, fueled processes of capitalist transformation that have dramatically accentuated class differences with a rapidity for which few were prepared;

and second, the alienation of capital stock signifies no less than the alienation of profits.

In any event, the honeymoon (such as it was) proved to be all too short. The collapse of communism resulted in the implosion of existing institutions, and it would take years before new institutions could be established and stabilized. In the meantime, local mafias grew rich while foreign investors bought up much of the economy. Pyramid schemes wiped out the savings of ordinary citizens in Romania and Albania. Corruption and cronyism came to plague much of the region. Trading patterns established for nearly half a century were disrupted and altered. In all the countries of the region there were initial contractions in industrial production, producing deep recession and radically changing the class composition of these societies. In Hungary, industrial production contracted at a rate of nearly 20% annually for three years; in Poland, the same annual rate of contraction was maintained for two years. In the Czech Republic, national income declined by nearly 25% annually for three years. Rates of contraction were also severe in the Balkans.[14] Gross domestic product declined over the years 1990–93 by annual average rates of 11.5% in Bulgaria, 6.6% in the Czech Republic, 5.0% in Hungary, 4.2% in Poland, 10.3% in Romania, 8.0% in Slovakia, and 4.9% in Slovenia—with more catastrophic declines in the Balkan war zone.[15] In 1991, just two years after communism collapsed in much of the region, rates of unemployment had risen in most of the region and, aside from Bulgaria, where unemployment was officially registered at 3.4%, rates of joblessness ranged from 5.6% in Czechoslovakia to a high of 15% in Yugoslavia (see table 3.1). Then unemployment rose throughout the region in the early 1990s, while the U.N. Economic Commission for Europe warned that the region was "sliding into a depression comparable with that experienced by the West between 1929 and 1933."[16] Production sank by an average of 20% in 1991 alone, resulting in further losses of jobs.[17] As of 1995, only the Czech Republic and Romania recorded unemployment rates of less than 10%. Elsewhere in the region, unemployment ranged from a low of 10.9% in Hungary to a high of 37.7% in Macedonia, with unemployment rates in Albania, Croatia, and the Federal Republic of Yugoslavia all recorded, officially at least, above 15%.[18] Large sectors of the population were driven into poverty (see table 3.2). As of 1999/2000, 64.5% of Serbs, 65% of Romanians, and 30% of Albanians lived below the poverty line, and 76% of Bulgarians polled (in January 1999) said that they lived in poverty.[19] Western products flooded the region, resulting in serious trade deficits and rising indebtedness. With

TABLE 3.1

Unemployment Levels in Eastern Europe Shortly after the Collapse of Communism

Country	% Unemployed (1991)
Albania	9.1
Bulgaria	3.4
Czechoslovakia	5.6
Hungary	8.5
Poland	11.8
Romania	8.7
Yugoslavia	15

SOURCE: Bulgaria, calculated from information provided in Bulgarian Telegraph Agency, 22 August 1991, in *BBC Summary of World Broadcasts,* 5 September 1991; Czechoslovakia, CSTK (Prague), 3 December 1991, in *BBC Summary of World Broadcasts,* 12 December 1991; Yugoslavia, *Economist,* 29 October 1988, 52, all via www.lexisnexis.com/academic/universe/; all other countries, UN Department of Economic and Social Affairs, Statistics Division—Statistical Databases (Georgetown University databases).

these considerations in mind, Poznański assessed the postcommunism transition in Eastern Europe as a failure.[20] Today, with several of the countries in the region already admitted to the European Union and NATO, and others hopeful of admission, the picture looks different. But the difficulties encountered in the first years of transition and the decisions taken in meeting them will prove to have made a long-lasting difference for the future of the region's countries.

The transfer of local stock to foreign control may be hard to reverse, for example. By the turn of the century, 70% of Hungary's industry and banking and essentially all printed media were foreign owned; 35% of Polish industry and 50% of Polish banking, together with 30% of Czech industry and 25% of Czech banking, were also foreign owned, and the tendency was toward ever greater portions of local industry and banking coming under foreign control.[21] By early 2000, moreover, some 75% of printed media in Poland was foreign owned, together with essentially all printed media in Bulgaria.[22] Macedonia's capital stock was sold at a discount (as was Poland's), with Greek business concerns accounting for some 90% of foreign investments in the country.[23] This trend has continued and, in recent transactions, the Swedish firm Skanska purchased a 75% share in the Polish firm

TABLE 3.2

Poverty Levels in Eastern Europe at the Collapse of Communism

Country	% below poverty line	Year
Albania	N/A	—
Bulgaria	>25	1992
Czechoslovakia	10	1992
Hungary	20–40	1989–90
Poland	20	late 1980s
Romania	20	early 1990s
Yugoslavia	25	late 1980s

SOURCE: Bulgaria, *Straits Times*, 13 January 1992, on Dow Jones and Reuters, *faktiva*; Czechoslovakia, *Toronto Star*, 9 February 1992, *faktiva*; Hungary, *New York Times*, 6 October 1989, and Hungarian Telegraph Agency (Budapest), 30 May 1990, at www.lexisnexis .com/academic/universe/; Romania, International Fund for Agricultural Development, *Romania: Country Strategic Opportunities Paper* (Rome, 9–10 April 2003); and Poland and Yugoslavia, *Poverty in Poland, Hungary, and Yugoslavia in the Years of Crisis, 1978–87* (Washington D.C.: World Bank, Policy Research Working Paper Series, no. 507), at www .ideas.repec.org/p/wbk/wbrwps/507.html (accessed 16 February 2006).

Exbud; Ferrovial of Spain bought up 50% of the shares of Poland's second largest construction firm, Budimex; France's TAIAcom acquired a 35% stake in Telekommunikacja Polska SA; global venture firm Advent International purchased Bolix, a Polish insulation manufacturer, as well as Terapia, a Romanian pharmaceutical company; Deutsche Telecom has invested considerable funds in the mobile phone company Polska Telefonya Cyfrowa; and Citigroup won a mandate for utility privatization in Hungary.[24] Even Kosovo and the Republika Srpska, former war zones, have put companies up for sale in hopes of reviving their economies.[25] Although most of the initial foreign investments came from West European firms, South Korea's automaking giant, Daewoo Corporation, also joined the investment frenzy, pouring billions of dollars into local auto manufacturers by the end of the 1990s,[26] while Bulgarian émigrés took advantage of the new atmosphere to invest in their home country.[27] There has also been some intraregional investment, such as the Hungarian bid to purchase an 89.4% stake in Serbia's Niska banka in 2005.[28]

By spring 2005, with the admission of Poland, the Czech Republic, Slovakia, Hungary, and Slovenia to the European Union, there was renewed optimism about the region. The *Times* of London reported in May of that year, for example, that the Czech Republic and Hungary had experienced record growth in the stock market, while the other countries in the region had experienced modest but respectable growth. Although the paper speculated that economic growth may have peaked in the region, the *Times* noted that the new EU members were "becoming increasingly attractive places for western firms to do business because many have lower corporate-tax rates and a cheaper workforce."[29] The following month, the *Economist* reported, in confirmation, that these countries, "though much poorer than France or Germany, are already a lot richer than they were immediately after communism's collapse."[30]

Undoubtedly, some of the economies in the region are sturdier and more productive today than they were at the end of the communist era. But, for ordinary working-class people, the key measures of success are employment and staying above the poverty line. On these two measures, the rosy picture sketched above looks murkier. Taking 1991 as the base line (table 3.1), we can see that rates of unemployment have increased (table 3.3) in Albania, Bulgaria, the Czech Republic, Slovakia, and Poland, while dipping slightly in Hungary from 8.5% in 1991 to 7.3% in 2005. In Yugoslavia, just before its breakup, the overall rate of unemployment was 15%; sixteen years later, the rate of joblessness is higher in several of the Yugoslav successor states, specifically the Bosnian Federation (43%), the Republika Srpska (38%), Croatia (19%), Kosovo (90% among Serbs, 70% among Albanians), Macedonia (37.5%), and Serbia (21.5%). Only in Slovenia is unemployment at a modest level (6.4%).

In terms of jobs, it would appear that the large volume of investments in the region has not made a decisive improvement for those at the lower end of the economic scale. On the other hand, comparing percentages of those living below the poverty line (tables 3.2, 3.4), it appears that there has been tangible improvement in Bulgaria, the Czech Republic, Hungary, and Poland, while the percentage of those living below the poverty line in Romania rose from 20% in the early 1990s to 28.9% in 2002. Albania, Croatia, and Macedonia also reported proportions greater than 25% of persons living below the poverty line. In essence, we see a mixed picture, with countries in the northern tier (including Slovenia) doing better than those in the southern tier, though with Bulgaria apparently doing better than any of its southern neighbors on these measures.

This rather mixed picture in terms of progress in reducing unemployment and poverty alerts us to the importance of the fact that, throughout the

TABLE 3.3

Unemployment Levels in Eastern Europe after Privatization

Country	% Unemployed	Year
Albania	14.6	2005
Bosnia-Herzegovina (Federation)	43	2003
Bosnia-Herzegovina (Republika Srpska)	38	2003
Bulgaria	9	2005
Croatia	19	2005
Czech Republic	8.9	2005
Hungary	7.3	2005
Kosovo (Serbs)	90	2004
Kosovo (Albanians)	70	2004
Macedonia	37.5	2005
Poland	17.2	2005
Romania	8.2	2005
Serbia	21.5	2004
Slovakia	16.1	2005
Slovenia	6.4	2005

SOURCE: Albania, *ATA News Agency* (Tirana), 25 May 2005; Bosnian Federation, *Onasa News Agency* (Sarajevo), 15 July 2003; Bosnia—Republika Srpska, *Onasa News Agency*, 28 December 2003; *HINA* (Zagreb), 21 February 2005; Czech Republic, *Deutsche Presse-Agentur* (Hamburg), 9 January 2006; Macedonia, *Makedonija Denes* (Skopje), 30 December 2005; Kosovo, *SRNA* (Bijeljina), 17 December 2004; Serbia, *Tanjug news agency* (Belgrade), 6 March 2004; all others, *Deutsche Presse-Agentur*, 2 February 2006, all via www.newsbank.com/govlib/awn.

region, it was not the EU model of mixed economy that predominated but a more purely capitalist model, in which rapid (re)privatization was often associated with corruption. In Poland, the outright purchase of Polish companies and their conversion into local affiliates of multinational corporations resulted in what Derek Monroe has called "a de facto 'Latin Americanization' of the Polish economy"—which is to say, foreign ownership of the key branches of industry, a growing gulf between the rich and the poor, and persistent problems of national indebtedness. As of 2005, moreover, the unemployment rate in Poland (19%) was more than double the EU average.[31]

There were some, such as Charles Gati, as well as the aforementioned Kepes, Bollobás, Tokay, and Tudoran, who feared from the beginning that

TABLE 3.4

Poverty Levels in Eastern Europe after Privatization

Country	% below Poverty Line	Year
Albania	25	2004
Bosnia-Herzegovina	18	2003
Bulgaria	12.8	2002
Croatia	29.2	2004
Czech Republic	3	2004
Hungary	12–13	2003
Macedonia	30.2	2003
Poland	12	2005
Romania	28.9	2002
Serbia and Montenegro	10	2003
Slovakia	20	2005
Slovenia	10	2003

SOURCE: Albania, Macedonia, Romania, Serbia and Montenegro, CIA, *The World Factbook,* at www.cia.gov/cia/publications/factbook/geos (accessed 18 December 2005); Bosnia-Herzegovina, *The World Bank: Bosnia and Herzegovina Country Brief 2005,* at www.worldbank.org (accessed 2 December 2005); Bulgaria, *The World Bank: Bulgaria Country Brief 2005,* at www.worldbank.org (accessed 18 December 2005); Croatia, Catholic sources as reported by *HINA* (Zagreb), 15 January 2005, at www.newsbank.com/govlib/awn; Czech Republic, *Prague Post,* 24 June 2004, at www.praguepost.com (accessed 19 December 2005); Hungary, *Budapest Sun,* 3 July 2003, at www.budapest.sun (accessed 19 December 2005); Poland, *Guardian* (London), 28 October 2005, at www.guardian.co.uk (accessed 18 December 2005); Slovakia, *Deutsche Presse-Agentur,* 9 November 2005, at www.lexisnexis.com/academic/universe/; and Slovenia, "at risk of poverty," in *Statistical Office of the Republic of Slovenia,* at www.stat.si/eng/tema-demografsko-zivljenska.asp (accessed 18 December 2005).

the transition might be derailed and end in political or economic debacle, if not both. But there were all too few who understood in advance (or, for that matter, who understand even now) that capitalism itself could assume a form inimical to the liberal project or who reflected on the fact that Eastern Europe was engaging in orchestrated repluralization at a time when, under the impact of Reagan, Thatcher, Kohl, and other governments, and continuing with both president Bush and British prime ministers Major and Blair, the West—and in particular the United States—was taking rapid strides from democracy to plutocracy, in essence reshaping the Western

model of pluralism. Viewed in this light, the transition from one-party socialism to plutocratic capitalism held, not the promise of the realization of
the liberal project, but only the certainty of a second betrayal (communism
having constituted the first betrayal)—indeed, a betrayal all the more bitter
because the plutocrats of the West continue to recite the old liberal truths,
which they themselves no longer fully honor.

In chapter 2, I defined classical liberalism as a value system based
on the concept of Natural Law (or Universal Reason) and centered on the
rule of law, notions of individual rights and duties, tolerance, respect for the
harm principle, equality, and the neutrality of the state in matters of religion. Rule of law entails that all laws be published, that there be no secret
legal codes or appendices, that the laws be applied equally to all citizens,
and that officeholders be equally subject to the law. Tolerance, further, is
not the same thing as indulgence, much less apathy. It is, on the contrary,
the active embrace of heterogeneity—perhaps especially in the cultural and
social spheres. This interfaces with capitalism when imported television
programming, films, music, and fashions threaten to overwhelm and suffo-
cate local manufactures, local culture, and local traditions.

The liberal principle of equality may also be marshaled to provide a
foundation for a critique of capitalism. While equality has been "interpreted
by those right of center as limited to mere legal or civic equality ('equal before the law'), [and] extended by the center to include also equality of opportunity (with attendant demands for 'affirmative action' and/or quotas),"
liberals on the left have insisted that equality counts as such only when progressive taxation is combined with levels of unemployment benefits, state-
funded medical care, and low-cost pharmaceuticals sufficient to eliminate
extremes of wealth and poverty.[32]

There are, of course, those who would agree with C. B. MacPherson
that what Locke achieved in his *Two Treatises of Government* "was to base
the property right on natural right and natural law, and then to remove all
the natural law limits from the property right."[33] On the other hand, there is
this striking passage in the *Second Treatise*:

> For he that leaves as much as another can make use of, does as good
> as take nothing at all. No Body could think himself injur'd by the
> drinking of another Man, though he took a good Draught, who had a
> whole River of the same Water left to him to quench his thirst. And
> the Case of Land and Water, *where there is enough of both*, is perfectly
> the same.[34]

My own view is that Locke's defense of the right of property acquisition (written to address the enclosure controversy) was qualified by two considerations: equality and sufficiency. In a word, no person or corporation or conglomerate may hold (or enclose) so much property as to render it unlikely that others will still find enough property for the satisfaction of their basic needs. Moreover, implicit here is a notion of minimal property, and "minimal" means necessary to live on a level that could be construed as being in harmony with the dual principles of equality and sufficiency. There is, in short, a "left" interpretation of Locke, and of the liberal tradition more broadly.[35]

More than two centuries after the death of Locke, that great British liberal thinker L. T. Hobhouse argued for the internal coherence of a liberal socialism (what we would call "social democracy" today). In *Liberalism* (1911), Hobhouse went much further than Locke in urging, first, that "freedom is only one side of social life" and must be counterbalanced by "mutual aid," and, second, that vast inequalities of wealth are, on the face of things, problematic for the liberal project and can be justified only if the continuation of such inequalities can be shown to be "better for the good *of all*."[36] For Hobhouse, all wealth is ultimately social wealth, that is, wealth made possible by social organization and legitimated only to the extent that it serves to advance the common good; from this postulate, Hobhouse concluded that all persons have a right to own property and, more controversially, that remuneration should be commensurate with productive work. Not surprisingly, Hobhouse expressed contempt for investors who made a living exclusively from buying and selling stocks.[37] Those familiar with Pope Leo XIII's *Rerum novarum* will readily see some commonality between Hobhouse's tract and the pontiff's encyclical, issued twenty years earlier.

It follows that classical liberalism is not necessarily as friendly toward laissez-faire capitalism, let alone plutocratic forms of government, as is sometimes thought, and that capitalism, where it does injury to the principles of equality and sufficiency, or to the harm principle, figures as an antiliberal force. The term "liberal economics" as it is customarily used is in fact an oxymoron, because the liberal project can be protected only—as James Madison and Thomas Jefferson understood—where the state is harnessed to protect the poor and the weak from the rich and even, I reiterate, to set limits on the accumulation of wealth. Where the state is harnessed to protect the privileges of the rich, one has neither liberalism nor democracy. This is why I have suggested that only an economic system based on the dual principles of free enterprise and state regulation of income and property can be considered legitimate.[38] I call this economic system *solidarism* and contrast it with the rival illegitimate systems, capitalism and socialism.

I make no claim to originality in espousing this interpretation, for which I am indebted to that other vehicle of Natural Law teachings: the papal encyclicals of the Catholic Church, above all Pope Leo XIII's *Rerum novarum* (1891), Pope John XXIII's *Mater et magistra* (1961), and Pope John Paul II's *Sollicitudo rei socialis* (1988) and *Centesimus Annus* (1991).[39] In the last-mentioned encyclical, Pope John Paul II urged that

> error consists in an understanding of human freedom which detaches itself from obedience to the truth, and consequently from the duty to respect the rights of others. The essence of freedom then becomes self-love carried to the point of contempt for God and neighbor, a self-love which leads to an unbridled affirmation of self-interest and which refuses to be limited by any demand.[40]

This translucent passage captures much of the reason for the deep disappointment many East Europeans have felt in the transition (or transformation) process.

There are at least two reasons why many self-professed liberals have been willing to countenance the scourges of vast economic inequality in supposedly liberal societies. The first is that not all liberals accept the Natural Law tradition. Many, including distinguished ethicist L. W. Sumner and articulate philosopher Russell Hardin, subscribe to that alternative current, *consequentialism*.[41] And, while I respect the sophistication of their work and have benefited from it, I fear that consequentialism is a poor guide to social policy and, indeed, that it may offer a framework within which the alleged costs of "progress" may more easily be justified. The second reason is that there has been a general assumption that what passes under the term "economic liberalism" must, of necessity, be compatible with political liberalism, indeed with any strain of political liberalism.[42] For "economic liberals," the favored recipe is a minimalist state in which, especially in post-Reagan, post-Thatcher economics—the rich and the prosperous are expected to contribute ever smaller amounts in taxes, in hopes that their prosperity will "trickle down" to the indigent for whom, in the meantime, most social services have been eliminated or cut back in order to keep the shrinking budget balanced. On this point, *Centisimus Annus* comments: "The State cannot limit itself to 'favoring one portion of the citizens,' namely the rich and prosperous, nor can it 'neglect the other,' which clearly represents the majority of society. Otherwise, there would be a violation of that law of justice [Natural Law] which ordains that every person should receive his due."[43]

There are, no doubt, some who feel that the liberal state ought not to get involved in trying to foster social justice, who feel that it is enough that the state not interfere in the freedom of citizens to do as they please, who feel that it is not the state's role, for example, to fund rehabilitation programs or low-cost, high-quality public education, even if those services might expand the range of the effective freedom of less prosperous citizens. Such sentiments are often associated with a relativism rooted not in true tolerance but in apathy. But apathy is completely foreign to the Natural Law tradition, and, as Polish sociologist Jerzy Szacki has urged, "liberalism is not identical with moral relativism and does not call upon its followers to accord equal value to all conceptions. There are not and cannot be any liberals who would be neutral in this sense."[44] Or, to put it another way, there are some behaviors that ought not to be tolerated in a liberal society.

Keeping in mind the sundry points made in this chapter, it is clear that, with the exception of the Czech Republic and Slovenia, the postcommunist societies of Eastern Europe have not been building liberal democracies at all; rather, they have been constructing hybrids in which some liberal and democratic elements are blended into a fundamentally plutocratic-colonial structure. And, as against the moral universalism entailed in the Natural Law tradition, some of these societies have been embracing conventionalism (with its tendencies toward the absolutization of the laws) and consequentialism (including in its most virulent form, chauvinistic nationalism). Here I note Zdeněk Suda's recent warning that nationalism, in the East European area, "has been so powerful a foe that even today it might be premature to consider the victory of liberalism as final."[45] I explore the philosophical roots of the relationship between nationalism and liberal democracy in the next chapter.

4

THREE VIEWS OF
SOVEREIGNTY
The East European Connection

I alluded in chapter 3 to the threat nationalism may pose to the liberal project, hinting that I consider a nationalism that claims differential rights for members to be incompatible with the Natural Law tradition or, as it is sometimes called, the tradition of Universal Reason. There are, to be sure, "liberal nationalists"[1] who argue that nationalism may provide a basis for group solidarity, thereby fostering the very principle of solidarism described briefly in chapter 3. But there are both theoretical and practical reasons to resist the temptation to marry liberalism to national feeling. On a theoretical level, national feeling involves a collective bond among persons sharing the same language or culture, a bond which, to the extent that it becomes primary, displaces the human solidarity prescribed by the Natural Law tradition and entailed in the liberal project. On a practical level, as Jamie Mayerfeld has pointed out, "because . . . nationalism impairs people's ability to form an accurate moral evaluation of their own nation's conduct, it often leads them to excuse the unjustifiable use of violence." Indeed, Mayerfeld goes further, arguing that "*any* nationalism, liberal or otherwise, will exert pressure on people to undertake, in the name of the nation, acts of violent aggression or violent resistance that are unjust even according to non-controversial and minimally complete standards of morality."[2] The decade of interethnic violence in the western Balkans is a case in point.

At the heart of the controversy about the relationship of nationalism to liberal democracy is the sometimes slippery concept of *popular sovereignty,* as well as the choice of balance to be struck between the rule of law and majority rule. In the years since 1987, and especially during the transformative years 1987–90, the notion of popular sovereignty has repeatedly been asserted in Eastern Europe, always with the certainty that this notion bears an unproblematic, uncontestable, and ultimately simple relation to democracy, in the generally understood meaning of that latter term—that is, rule by the people as exercised through the medium of representative government. Popular sovereignty has further been so closely associated with the doctrine of national self-determination as to lead many political actors and observers alike to consider them inseparable. These twin convictions have colored the political transformations in the region over the past decade, infusing nationalist suppositions with the aura of a legitimacy of which they do not, in fact, partake.

The democratic tradition, however, as I argue here, admits of at least three rather different views of sovereignty: the conventionalist-realist view (traceable to Hobbes), the universalist-idealist view (advanced by Kant), and the nationalist symbiosis (which might be traced to Herder but which must, more properly, be associated with the political impulses and ideological currents spawned by the French philosophes and popularized by the French Revolution). One could, of course, easily add to this list by identifying the specific strain of liberal-idealism defended by Locke (and, in calling him an idealist, I am thinking of his emphasis on Natural Law as the ultimate source of both duty and right) or the "rational realism" of Hegel, who tied obligation to the interdependence of family, community, and state, rather than to some overarching ideal that might take the form of a categorical imperative, and placed sovereignty unambiguously within the normative framework of the state, rather than ascribe it to popular will à la Rousseau. And, no doubt, other variations might occur to one or another observer. However, the three views I have identified represent the most important, most influential, and hence also the most potent alternatives in post-1989 Eastern Europe; other views or interpretations are either variations of these three or less potent permutations lacking real influence in the region.

LIBERAL REALISM: HOBBES'S ABSOLUTE SOVEREIGNTY

Thomas Hobbes (1588–1679) bears a problematic relationship to the classical liberal tradition. On one hand, one may note his subscription to notions of Natural Law,[3] his belief that the central purpose of political authority is the maintenance of civil order (a belief he shares with others whose liberal credentials are unchallenged), and the fact that he viewed the individual as possessing at least one inalienable right—the right to life. Hobbes was, on the other hand, no champion of democracy. He was a champion of monarchy, but his priority was not monarchy as such but effective government, and for him any effective government that could assure civil order was better than an ineffective government, no matter how noble its ideals or radiant its institutions.[4] To the extent that Hobbes was convinced of the natural superiority of monarchy over democracy,[5] it was because he judged monarchy to be better equipped to maintain civil order.

As Leo Strauss has pointed out, Hobbes undertook to reconcile two rival theories of sovereignty: *patrimonialism,* which traced sovereignty to the rights of fathers (or husbands) over other members of their families, and *contract theory,* which held that legitimate authority could be premised only on the voluntary submission of free citizens.[6] Hobbes broke with tradition by exalting the state over the Church, demanding that religion serve the interests of the state. In his *Dialogue between a Philosopher and a Student,* as in his *Leviathan,* Hobbes demanded obedience and assent to the laws and decrees of government, saying nothing of any right of rebellion.[7] On the contrary, the only "inalienable" right Hobbes allows a person, even in defiance of sovereign authority, is the right to protect his own life.[8]

In taking this harsh view, Hobbes was responding to the political uncertainties and ideological ferment unleashed by the English civil war. It was, indeed, the roundheads who, in the course of their war against the king, had laid the basis for establishing popular sovereignty as the ultimate authority in the land, that is, even over the king. But the roundheads were not thinking of people as such, of ordinary citizens organizing themselves as they might, but of the Parliament, or more specifically the "Long Parliament," as the embodiment of popular sovereignty.[9] Inevitably, the royalists countered that if the people were truly sovereign, then they could depose the Parliament and endorse the authority of the king.

Hobbes's response was to equate "the sovereign" with "the people" and to judge that any aggregation of rebels can constitute only "the crowd"—a group of individuals. He argued in *De Cive* (1642) that "a crowd cannot make a promise or an agreement, acquire or transfer a right, do, have, possess, and so on, except separately or as individuals, so that there are as many promises, agreements, rights, and actions, as there are men.

For this reason, a crowd is not a natural person."[10] It follows that, if no number of rebels can ever claim to constitute a "natural person"—a body able to claim rights—then there can never be a right of rebellion.

For Hobbes, then, the people are not sovereign; rather, the sovereign is the people. This might appear to be an inverted theory of popular sovereignty. But in fact it is not that at all, for in Hobbes's view sovereignty does not exist before the creation of government; it is, rather, a characteristic of government, not a power whereby government is created.[11] Nor could there be any appeal to a social contract, since, in Hobbes's view, the sovereign "was above the contract, as he was above any particular interpretation of divine, natural, or civil law other than his own."[12] The sovereign was, accordingly, the quintessential embodiment of freedom, in Hobbes's view.

Hobbes insisted that sovereignty had to be, perforce, *absolute* and *indivisible,* understanding by the former that the sovereign should rein supreme in the religious sphere, dictating which doctrines would be endorsed and which disallowed and prescribing ecclesiastical rituals for the society. On Hobbes's view, then, the sovereign "has the right both to decide which opinions and doctrines are inimical to peace and to forbid their being taught."[13] Perhaps paradoxically, Hobbes insisted nonetheless that sovereigns were bound by Natural Law,[14] but he resolved the moral dilemma of citizens placed under simultaneous obligation to obey both immoral commands of an absolute sovereign and the dictates of right reason by urging citizens confronting such a dilemma to choose (passive) civil disobedience and be prepared to endure martyrdom.[15] He resolved the dilemma of how the sovereign could be simultaneously absolute and subject to the Natural Law by deciding that it was up to the sovereign to interpret Natural Law for his society.

As Arnold Rogow notes, Hobbes cannot, in any way, be associated with the prehistory of either fascism or Marxism-Leninism, let alone Naziism, since his objective was clearly the protection of life and limb.[16] Moreover, where fascism and Naziism figure as manifestations of "mass politics," Hobbes's concept of the sovereign state reflects precisely his fear of the consequences of the mobilization of the masses. As for democracy, on the other hand, Hobbes was pointedly indifferent to its charms.

POPULIST DEMOCRACY: ROUSSEAU AND THE FRENCH REVOLUTION

Jean-Jacques Rousseau (1712–78) died eleven years before the outbreak of the French Revolution. But he was, in many ways, its spiritual godfather,

and his ideas about the General Will and about the primacy of the collective over the individual were fully embodied in the revolution. A radical egalitarian, Rousseau was an enthusiast for democracy, trusting implicitly to the
wisdom of the people. "The first thing the legislator must know," said Robe-
spierre, following Rousseau, "is that le peuple is good."[17]

Although there is a broad consensus that Rousseau was, in some
sense, a democrat,[18] it is a striking fact that Rousseau never advocated universal suffrage or even universal male suffrage.[19] Rousseau, who held that
sovereignty was originally invested in the people, who could never renounce
or alienate their fundamental sovereignty, drew a distinction between the
constitution of the state, which should be democratic, and the government, which—in his view—need not be democratic.[20] This is, perhaps,
why J. W. Chapman concludes that Rousseau wanted "to achieve liberal
ideas by totalitarian means."[21] Moreover, Rousseau, the advocate of unlim-
ited, indivisible, and "indestructible" popular sovereignty,[22] provided arguments that could readily be adduced in support of J. L. Talmon's thesis that
what Rousseau wanted could best be called "totalitarian democracy."[23] In
his demand that the individual accept the General Will as the embodiment
of her/his own interests, Rousseau anticipated Trotsky's later lament, "One
cannot be right against the party."

With the unfolding of the French Revolution, the Directorate's oper-
ationalization of Rousseau's formulae for populist democracy became wedded to a popular, messianic nationalism in which error was excluded by definition. Rousseau, for his part, was prepared to admit that people might be
deceived, but he insisted all the same that "the general will is always right
and ever tends to the public advantage"[24]—a monumental claim, as monumental as the contemporary faith in the ability of the market to respond to
the challenges of environmental destruction, the accelerating extinction
of species, overfishing, the spoliation of coral reefs, and overpopulation.
Rousseau, thus, was quite content to demand "the complete alienation by
each associate member to the community of *all his rights*."[25] Rousseau res-
cued the right of popular revolt from the absolutist state he justified, however, by the appeal to the doctrine of popular sovereignty, under which, in
his words, "government can be legitimate only on condition that each suc-
cessive generation of subjects is free either to accept or to reject it."[26]

Hence, although neither Hobbes nor Rousseau was a nationalist as
such, nationalism could find fertile soil only in the latter's thought, not in
the Hobbesian legacy. Hobbes, the conventionalist, was neither a liberal
nor a democrat, but he exerted influence on liberal democratic traditions

subsequently; Rousseau, the radical egalitarian, nonetheless advocated the establishment of a state religion, and, in spite of his advocacy of most of the liberal values, has had only covert influence: there are no Rousseauians in the world of politics.

John Locke, by contrast, was the first to propose a marriage of liberalism and democracy, but there have continued to be charges that the marriage is unstable. With organized groups, whether of the religious right or of corporate interests, for example, forever trying to scupper liberal values and transform democracy into a government of some of the people, by some of the people, for some of the people, with the former aspiring to erect a "republic of virtue" on the field of a victorious campaign against perceived vices,[27] there have inevitably been expressions of concern that democracy could degenerate into a tyranny of the majority, could become the vehicle for falsehood rather than truth, trample on minority cultures and traditions, and abolish the individual rights of people who find themselves in a minority on any of a number of vectors, whether confessional or sexual or racial or even class.[28] But, as Ian Shapiro has reminded us,[29] and in spite of examples of democratic intolerance, such as George W. Bush's advocacy of a constitutional amendment to outlaw gay/lesbian marriage, thereby relegating gays and lesbians to permanent second-class status, democracy has proven, historically, to be the most trustworthy vessel for liberal values and the surest guarantor of truth, individual rights, and, within some parameters, the flourishing of minority cultures. The success of the Lockean formula depends, as Locke knew but as many liberals today forget, on assuring that active citizens are educated, and, specifically, educated in the spirit of liberalism. Where this is not the case, liberal democracy may decay, transmogrifying into that cheap alloy, illiberal democracy, with its "bacchanalian revel"—to steal a phrase from Hegel—of persecutions, discrimination, and self-seeking.

I should record one final point before relinquishing our discussion of Rousseau. Jean-Jacques Rousseau is, for perfectly good reasons, routinely associated with notions of majority rule and, accordingly, democracy,[30] but, at the same time, he was quite explicit about his belief that "democracy is best suited to small states, aristocracy to those of medium size, and monarchy to the largest."[31] Here it is important to return to Rousseau's distinction between the (necessarily democratic) constitution of the state and its (not necessarily democratic) government. Hence, for Rousseau, there was nothing self-contradictory about the notion of an authoritarian democracy.

LIBERAL IDEALISM:
KANT'S DEFENSE OF LIBERAL MONARCHY

Immanuel Kant (1724–1804) bridled at the apparently authoritarian implications of Rousseau's theory. Indeed, Kant argued that direct democracy "is
necessarily a *despotism,* because it establishes an executive power through
which all the citizens may make decisions about [and indeed against] the
single individual without his consent . . . ; and this means that the general
will is in contradiction with itself, and thus also with freedom."[32] Thus, Kant
felt, the problem with democracy was that one could not rely on it to be liberal, Shapiro's more recent ruminations notwithstanding; and it was the
safeguarding of liberal values (rule of law, individual freedom, equality, tolerance, the autonomy of the individual) that mattered most to Kant. Indeed,
Kant was convinced that a (hereditary) monarchy was better equipped (and
hence more likely) to protect human rights than was a democracy, and
hence more compatible with the liberal tradition, properly understood. Kant
consistently praised what he called "republican government," but by that expression he was referring not to the structure of government but to its values. Accordingly, in a lesser-known work, Kant advises: "It is . . . the duty of
monarchs, even if they rule *autocratically,* to govern in a *republican* (not a
democratic) manner—that is, to treat the people in a manner consistent
with the spirit of the laws of freedom (as a people with fully developed reason would direct itself)."[33] On the other hand, Kant declares his conviction,
in his essay "Perpetual Peace," that "any form of government which is not
representative is essentially an *anomaly,* [while] . . . the other two political
constitutions [i.e., autocracy and aristocracy] are always defective."[34]

Given his strong disagreements with Rousseau, it is somewhat sur-
prising to discover some parallels between the two men on the subject of
sovereignty. First, in a manner reminiscent of Rousseau, Kant distinguishes
between the form of sovereignty, which might be autocratic, aristocratic, or
democratic, and the form of government, which relates to the organization
of power and needs to entail the separation of legislative and executive
power.[35] Second, in common with both Locke and Rousseau, Kant links the
establishment of state sovereignty to the need to protect property rights.[36]

In view of Kant's unmistakable commitment to liberal values, many
authors, including the present writer,[37] have had problems with the following passage in the *Metaphysics of Morals:*

> The head of a state has only rights against his subjects and no duties
> (that he can be coerced to fulfill). Moreover, even if the organ of the

head of a state, the *ruler,* proceeds contrary to law, for example, if he goes against the law of equality in assigning the burdens of state in matters of taxation, recruiting and so forth, subjects may indeed oppose this injustice by *complaints (gravamina)* but not by resistance. . . . A people cannot offer any resistance to the legislative head of a state that would be consistent with right, since a rightful condition is possible only by submission to its general legislative will. There is, therefore, no right to *sedition (seditio),* still less to *rebellion (rebellio).*[38]

Where Rousseau demanded the individual's unconditional submission to the General Will, Kant demands the unconditional submission of both the individual and any group to the government. Thus, for Kant, any notion of a "general will" is simply irrelevant.

But Kant does not follow Hobbes either. The Hobbesian monarch is credited with absolute sovereignty, but Kant repudiates such absolutism, insisting that insofar as subjects have inalienable rights, the ruler is obliged to respect those rights. The key qualifying phrase in the passage quoted above from the *Metaphysics of Morals* is "duties that he can be coerced to fulfill." It is not that the sovereign has no duties, only—for Kant—that no one has the right to coerce the sovereign to fulfill those duties (because the right to coerce the sovereign would erect a higher authority over and above the sovereign—which, in Kant's view and in a manner strangely reminiscent of Hobbes, would entangle one in self-contradiction). Kant does not require obedience to the unjust commands of a tyrant. On the contrary, he expressly permits and counsels disobedience to the sovereign in instances where obedience would require that the subject commit unjust or immoral acts. But resistance and rebellion are excluded.[39] And though Kant may agree with Hobbes in delegitimating rebellion, they differ in the role assigned to the sovereign. Where Hobbes assigns the sovereign the primary role of protecting people from each other[40] on the assumption that conflict is sown into human nature itself, Kant characterizes good government as "a maternal womb"[41] and is "interested in the devices nature uses to develop cooperative capacities, such as those needed to establish a law-governed civil order."[42]

THE CASE OF EASTERN EUROPE

As Donald Kommers and W. J. Thompson note, Kantian philosophy exerts tangible influence in contemporary constitutional development, above all in Europe, Kant's rigorous rationality holding a particular attraction for constitution framers.[43] But in Eastern Europe concepts of "national democracy," even of a neo-Rousseauian mold, have had their attraction—for example, in Croatia in the 1990s and in Serbia since 1987. This has less to do with "primordial sentiments" of ancient vintage or with a recrudescence of collective irrationality, as some observers would have it, than with two other factors. First, as the communist order dissolved, local elites saw in nationalism a means of sustaining their hold on power.[44] Second, for new states in the region (Slovenia, Croatia, Serbia, Montenegro, Macedonia, Estonia, Latvia, Lithuania, Belarus, Ukraine, and Moldova), nationalism seemed to be essential in drawing the borders of the community. Montenegro's vote to separate from Serbia (in May 2006) may have referred to the republic's history of independence, but it was motivated in the first place by the desire to escape Serbia's dysfunctional politics.

A comparison of the constitutions of ten of the postcommunist states in the region (all except Albania and Bosnia-Herzegovina) bears out my claim that concepts of national democracy have been influential in the region. Specifically, all of them except the incomplete Polish constitutional act of October 17, 1992 make reference to either popular sovereignty or national sovereignty. The Bulgarian constitution declares, for example, that "the entire power of the state shall derive from the people" (Article 2), while the Czech constitution of 1992 declares (Article 2) that "the people shall be the source of all power in the state."[45] The Macedonian constitution follows this mold, prescribing that "Sovereignty in the Republic of Macedonia derives from the citizens and belongs to the citizens" (Article 2). And again, in the constitution of the Republic of Hungary, one finds the affirmation (in Article 2), "In the Republic of Hungary, all power shall belong to the people exercising its sovereignty through its elected representatives as well as directly." Only the Czech constitution adds the explanation, "A constitutional law may determine the instances when the people are to exercise state power directly."

We have already seen that, in the Hobbesian concept, popular sovereignty has no meaning, indeed no existence, after the founding of the state. The constitutions of Hungary, Macedonia, and the Czech Republic are, accordingly, not Hobbesian in spirit; in fact, they are closer to Rousseau. For Kant, moreover, "popular sovereignty" is a misnomer, since sovereignty, in Kant's view, is an aspect and dimension of government and therefore cannot exist prior to the founding of government. For Kant, it follows that government can neither alienate nor transfer sovereignty; thus, sovereignty has nothing to do with the people, the nation, or any other collectivity of persons. On the contrary, sovereignty is what makes government, government.

That said, the foregoing constitutions are nonetheless somewhat closer than those of other states in the region to the liberal spirit, and the Bulgarian constitution's requirement that the state "assist in the maintenance of tolerance and respect among the believers from different denominations, and among believers and non-believers" (Article 37) is closer to Locke than to either Hobbes or Rousseau. By contrast with the foregoing, however, the constitutions of Croatia, Serbia, Slovenia, Slovakia, and Romania seek legitimation by asserting specifically national sovereignty, though only the Croatian, Serbian, and Romanian constitutions establish "national states" as such. The constitution of the Republic of Serbia (adopted on September 28, 1990), for instance, describes the republic as "the state of the Serb people,"[46] while that of the Republic of Croatia represents that republic as "the national state of the Croatian nation and a state of members of other nations and minorities who are citizens," naming the Serbs first among those "other nations" (Preamble). The Croatian constitution's further elaboration that "the sovereignty of the Republic of Croatia is inalienable, indivisible, and untransferable" (Article 2) had the intended effect of rendering local Serb separatism unconstitutional. The Croatian constitution based itself, at the very outset, on what it called "the Croatian nation's historical right to full sovereignty." In 2000, however, the newly elected Croatian government headed by Prime Minister Ivica Račan and President Stipe Mesić opened the question of redefining Croatia as a "citizens' state" (in which all citizens are fully equal) rather than a national state (with vague suggestions that the dominant nation is to be favored).[47]

The Romanian constitution of December 1991 is also in this "national" mold, affirming, in Article 2, "National sovereignty resides with the Romanian people, who shall exercise it through its representative bodies and by referendum." Ultimately, the Romanian constitution, like the constitution of Macedonia, straddles the fence. We thus find Article 4 of Romania's constitution declaring that "Romania is the common and indivisible homeland of all its citizens," though the word "indivisible" was chosen to delegitimate any lingering Hungarian irredentist or autonomist fantasies in connection with Transylvania. Macedonia's constitution, while emphasizing civil equality, also pays obeisance, in the preamble, to "the historical fact that Macedonia is established as a national state of the Macedonian people," as part of a compromise formula devised to purchase the support of the right.[48] The constitutions of Slovenia and Slovakia also pay obeisance, in passing, to the national principle, by way of justifying their acts of disociation from their respective federations, but both declare themselves "democratic" states, rather than "national" states, with the Slovenian document even adding, "Slovenia is a state of all its citizens" (Article 3).

I stated at the outset that the Lockean concept of popular sovereignty is irrelevant to contemporary Eastern Europe. This might appear strange to some, however, in light of the supposed goals of the revolutions in the region (limited government, economic privatization, open borders). And it may be further supposed that not only the Bulgarian but also the Czech, Hungarian, and Slovak constitutions may be not just closer to Locke in certain particulars but fully within the Lockean tradition. After all, it was Locke who undertook the first endeavor to reconcile liberal values with limited government, and Locke also who offered an articulate liberal defense of rebellion against tyranny. But Locke's irrelevance may readily be demonstrated. To begin with, Locke placed his emphasis squarely on the protection of private property. He had the following to say about the purpose of government in his *First Treatise of Government*:

> Property, whose Original is from the Right a Man has to use any of the Inferior Creatures, for the Subsistence and Comfort of his Life, is for the benefit and sole Advantage of the Proprietor, so that he may even destroy the thing, that he has Property in by his use of it, where need requires: but *Government being for the Preservation of every Mans Right and Property,* by preserving him from the Violence and Injury of others, is for the good of the Governed.[49]

While all of these constitutions except that of the Czech Republic contain provisions guaranteeing the sanctity of private property, none of them represent the protection of private property as the central purpose of government, a construal that reduces popular sovereignty to a mere vehicle of property rights.

There is a further passage in Locke's *Two Treatises* worthy of attention, in the *Second Treatise*. Here Locke makes positive law contingent on its being in accord with Natural Law, stating the case more strongly than Kant would later. "The Municipal Laws of Countries," he writes there, "are only so far right, as they are founded on the Law of Nature, by which they are to be regulated and interpreted." Crediting Richard Hooker, Locke adds that "the Laws which have been hitherto mentioned, i.e., the Laws of Nature, do bind Men," which is to say also officeholders.[50] In so saying, Locke invites one to accept the notion of an external standard—Natural Law—by which the morality and justice of the state's legislative and policy acts may be judged. That no such external standard, located in human reason, is accorded a place in the constitutions of the postcommunist states of Eastern Europe goes without saying. These considerations incline me to consider Lockean theory largely unrepresented in the region in question. This is ironic given that the anticommunist dissidents of yesteryear held the socialist state to just such an external standard.

On the other hand, the Polish constitution of 1997 begins with the affirmation, "We, the Polish nation, all citizens of the Republic, equally those believing in God as the source of truth, goodness and beauty, and those not sharing that faith and drawing these universal truths from other sources, equal in their rights and duties toward Poland . . ."[51] This clause, together with a right-to-life affirmation, suggest that the Polish constitution, unlike the constitutions of other republics in the region, contains passages referring to Natural Law (here, under the term "universal truths"), but the inclusion of a reference to God makes clear that the constitution framers were alluding to Natural Law not only, or even primarily, as secular reason, but also, and even primarily, as the Law of God. Ironically, the text, which emerged as a compromise between the church and parties on the left in Poland, alienated Solidarity activists as well as some sectors of the church. Radio Marija, for example, condemned the constitution as "a threat to the Christian tradition of the Polish people."[52]

NATIONALISM AND SOVEREIGNTY

Many observers have commented on the proliferation of nationalist symbols, parties, actions, and violence in the region since the mid-1980s, predating, thus, the watershed year 1989. The most common explanation, especially in the popular mass media, has been that the nationalist sentiments were there all along but were merely held in check by the tough communist regimes. As those regimes weakened and then crumbled—so the refrain goes—nationalist sentiments rose to the surface.

This theory strikes me as too facile. A more sophisticated assessment has been offered by John Ishiyama and Markjke Breuning, who suggest that the psychological and social disorientation associated with the transition from authoritarian one-party rule to (albeit often corrupt) forms of pluralism naturally opened the door to "ethnopolitical extremism."[53] Jack

Snyder, as already noted, has connected the spiral of nationalism to elite manipulation.

To my mind, two further factors need to be taken into account. First, communism paradoxically not only reinforced and strengthened nationalism but even, in some instances, invented new nationalisms; Macedonia and Moldova come to mind, along with certain central Asian republics. The communist authorities of Eastern Europe were, of course, implacably hostile to everything that smacked of nationalism (except in the case of Romania) but—in contrast to the centralizing examples set by France, Spain, and Italy—adopted the practice of conceding territorial autonomy to ethnic minorities, whether one thinks of the USSR or Yugoslavia or Czechoslovakia or even, up to 1968, Romania. This practice could only serve to keep alive national identities and provide would-be separatists with vital institutional resources. In this regard, Romanian leader Nicolae Ceauşescu's abolition of the Magyar Autonomous Region in Romania in 1968 could be seen as a sensible prophylactic measure. But Ceauşescu made other concessions to nationalism, embracing Romanian nationalism and an adulatory approach to Romanian history as twin tools of legitimation.[54]

Second, as communism faded, the question "Who are we?" came to the fore, naturally and ineluctably. Communism's answer—"the working class"—was rejected, while answers referring to confessional identity were not even considered, for the most part. Instead, the answer was framed in terms of ethnolinguistic groups—nations—which, as often as not, crossed state frontiers. In eastern Germany, for example, huge crowds poured onto the streets of Berlin, Dresden, Leipzig, chanting, "Wir sind das Volk" (We are the people); but soon this chant became modified as "Wir sind ein Volk" (We are one people)—an allusion to their shared desire to overcome the division of Germany imposed by the Allies after World War II.[55]

In Yugoslavia, the challenge nationalism posed to state sovereignty was made quintessentially clear. The preservation of a united Yugoslavia had been premised on the inculcation of a limited sense of community, to which the label "Yugoslav socialist patriotism" had been affixed. But with the ascent of Milošević to power in Serbia and the rising tide of exclusivist and revanchist Serbian nationalism, non-Serbs felt threatened. More particularly, they felt threatened as non-Serbs and, one by one, began demanding either protection from Serbian authorities (via enhanced self-government) or dissociation from the federation. The first important statement to this effect, raising the banner of popular sovereignty, came in Slovenia, in the form of the officially sponsored "Fundamental Charter of

Slovenia" in spring 1989. Croatia, Bosnia-Herzegovina, and Macedonia also issued declarations of sovereignty before announcing their dissociation from the dying SFRY. In Serbia after 1987, Milošević authorized mass demonstrations by Serbs while disallowing mass demonstrations by Albanians, even where the latter had only the purpose of supporting the constitution. In this way, Milošević assumed a principle of popular sovereignty in which Serbs were equated with "the people" while Albanians were excluded from any part of "the people."

Taking stock of the region's record since 1989, it seems clear enough that Milošević (in Serbia), Mečiar (in Slovakia, until 1998), and Ion Iliescu (in Romania, holding office until 1996) were quite prepared to appeal to the "general will" to justify depredations against the rights of Albanians in Kosovo, Hungarians in southern Slovakia, or students and intellectuals in Romania. They seemed to operate in implicit, if not explicit, agreement with Sièyes's dictum that the will of the nation "is always lawful" since the nation "is herself the embodiment of the law"—or, to put it another way, above the law. In Rousseau's vision, as in that of Milošević or Mečiar (or Mayor Gheorghe Funar of Cluj, for that matter), Natural Law does not come into the picture: there is no categorical imperative other than the imperative (or rather, justification) to carry out a "general will" which is stoked and shaped by leaders with nationalist agendas.

CONCLUSION: HOPES FOR A MORE TOLERANT PARANOIA?

From the foregoing, I hope it is evident that there are both Rousseauian and Hobbesian elements in the political life of Eastern Europe—the former prevalent in much of the Balkans (albeit with a quasi-Hobbesian appeal to the supralegal status of the sovereign in the thinking of Milošević's supporters), and the spirit of the latter reflected, at least to some extent, in Hungary, the Czech Republic, post-Mečiar Slovakia, and in some ways also Bulgaria. I have described Slovenia, Macedonia, and Croatia as hybrids, though the "citizens" character is more pronounced in the Slovenian case (where the ideals of Kant arguably have come closest to realization), while the "national" character has been more pronounced in the case of Croatia, although (as already noted) the new government of 1999/2000 initiated processes intended to change the constitution in the direction of making it less "national."

I have also suggested that the East European states have confronted a choice among three models of sovereignty—the protoliberal absolutism of

Hobbes, the collectivist democratism of Rousseau, and the liberal monarchism of Kant—and have indicated why I believe that Locke's historically potent model is not available for practical adoption in the region. Of these four models, only that of Rousseau could be said to provide a fertile bed for nationalism.

Recently, the literature has seen an intense debate between liberal nationalists and liberal antinationalists. This debate is directly relevant to the political challenges being confronted in Eastern Europe. In brief, liberal nationalists consider it important for states to build a sense of shared national identity even in culturally diverse settings, while liberal antinationalists variously fear that such a result can be achieved only via oppressive measures or warn that the presumptions and claims of nationalists are at variance and in contradiction with the presumptions and values of liberals. Among the protagonists of a liberal nationalism are Liah Greenfeld,[56] Yael Tamir,[57] and Vladimir Tismaneanu.[58] Among the advocates of an antinationalist liberalism one may number Bernard Yack,[59] Iris Young,[60] Andrew Mason,[61] and Omar Dahbour,[62] as well as myself.[63] Mason offers practical considerations here, urging that "assimilation policies will have morally relevant costs, even if . . . these are not necessarily sufficient to justify speaking of oppression," and that, in any event, the advantages sought through the imposition of a common national identity might be obtainable "in other ways that do not impose the moral costs which arise from even moderate non-coercive assimilation policies."[64]

For my part, I am impressed by the albeit polemical definition of nationalism offered by Yugoslav novelist Danilo Kiš:

Nationalism is first and foremost paranoia, individual and collective paranoia. As collective paranoia it is the product of envy and fear and primarily the result of a loss of individual consciousness; it is nothing but a set of individual paranoias raised to the degree of paroxysm. . . . The nationalist is a frustrated individualist, nationalism the frustrated (collective) expression of his individualism, at once an ideology and [an] anti-ideology.[65]

The paranoia of nationalism is everywhere in evidence in post-1987–89 Eastern Europe—in Vladimir Dedijer's wide-eyed howling about a Vatican-Comintern conspiracy against Serbs, in István Csurka's excited admonitions about a capitalist-Jewish-Masonic conspiracy against Hungarians, in Vladimir Zhirinovsky's periodic rantings about the need for Slavs to band together in self-defense, in recurrent articles in Milošević's press in the late 1980s and early 1990s about Germany being a "Fourth Reich," and so forth. But insofar as liberal nationalists hope to tame the beast—rather than banish it—they end up seeking either to generate a nationalism that does not exclude anyone and is not directed against anyone—a nationalism that is not nationalism at all, as far as I can tell—or to produce some sort of tolerant strain of paranoia.

5

THE SO-CALLED RIGHT OF NATIONAL SELF-DETERMINATION AND OTHER MYTHS

The preceding chapter continued the discussion of nationalism, setting it in the context of alternative understandings of sovereignty. The analysis of nationalism would not be complete without a discussion of the central claim registered by nationalists, namely, that there is a universal, natural right of self-declared nations to be independent and to align the borders of the state with the territory inhabited by conationals. In a classic statement of this claim, Robert Redslob, a professor of the history of international law at the University of Strasbourg, wrote that "in a case of disparity between the nation and the State, a reorganization is legitimate, a reorganization which will be realized—by forceful or peaceful means—either by the foundation of a new State or by incorporation into an existing State with the same ethnic character."[1]

"Nations enjoy the right of self-determination"—so we have been told for so long that this affirmation appears, at least at first sight, to have as great a claim to certifiable veracity as the law of gravity. Even though complications and even conflicting claims are readily conceded, the principle seems to be beyond challenge, almost to enjoy status as a transcendent principle of political life. To the extent that a primary alternative receptacle of rights is identified, in the dominant liberal paradigm of the twentieth and early twenty-first centuries, that receptacle is the individual. And it is left to the state to resolve such differences and frictions as may arise between the rights enjoyed by individuals and the supposed rights of the nation.

Some of the confusion about this principle has to do with different concepts about the notion of "group rights." In agreement with Chandran Kukathas, I believe that groups of people have inherent rights as individuals and may enjoy negotiated or conventional rights as groups, although I would add that groups of people living in a community enjoy rights to services their government is obliged to provide. Will Kymlicka, whose ideas I take up in more detail shortly, believes that groups of people enjoy not only the aforementioned rights but also, in the case of cultural-linguistic groups, certain inherent rights that derive from their being a group with its own language and culture. In Kymlicka's view, this fact of cultural and linguistic specificity, endows the collective possessor with an inherent right to take such measures as are necessary to preserve its language and culture, even when those measures may limit the rights, within a designated zone, of other citizens of the state. Kymlicka's point of view may be justified or not, but it is not classical liberalism. And while few, if any, theorists would care to challenge the existence of group rights in the minimal sense Kukathas and I assign to the term—"group" being defined as any collectivity of persons associating on the basis of some common traits, interests, goals, or even hobbies,[2] and those rights derivable from the rights of individuals or from positive rights established by law—there have been controversies concerning the precise moral content, political nature, and limits of group rights. There are other complications, too, with the notion of national rights, and it will be seen that claims concerning national rights cannot be derived from those concerning group rights, since the former entail the notion that persons geographically or politically cut off from the nation are nonetheless "of the nation," participating fully in the rights of that nation and contributing, through their mere existence, to claims based on sheer number.

Although the doctrine of the right of national self-determination lacks any firm foundation, floating as it were in midair, rather like Rene Magritte's renowned depiction of a castle on a flying rock, the doctrine is assisted in its flight by two hot-air balloons: the myth of political realism, and the current warped proscription of values in the social sciences some writers would urge upon us under the banner of "complete liberty for scientific inquiry." The doctrine's advocates even argue on its behalf that it should be identified with majority rule and, via that principle, with democracy itself, even if the question within which boundaries the given majority is to be sought is, at times, not susceptible of adequate resolution—which is why the U.N. Charter (Article 5), despite its embrace of the principle of self-determination, carefully avoids specifying that this right is vested in nations.[3] Moreover, if it is democratic to be nationalist, does that mean that we may describe the excesses of nationalism as "excesses of democracy," as "too much democracy"? An answer in either the affirmative or the negative should sound simplistic, and it is so because the very identification of the national principle with democracy is itself simplistic.

MODERN MYTHOLOGY

In this section and the next two I summarize three contemporary myths about rights and then discuss the fatal flaws afflicting these myths. In the final section I propose an alternative theory of legitimacy and rights, based in large part on Kant's *Metaphysics of Morals* and on a previous book of my own.[4]

Myth 1: National self-determination. The central idea inspiring nationalism has remained remarkably constant since Johann Gottfried von Herder (1744–1803). It may be summed up in the demand that the state serve as the legal-institutional embodiment and protector of the nation and its culture.[5] This principle does not exclude the possibility of there being two equally legitimate Hungarian states, or two Romanian national states, or two German states, or even a multiplicity of states identified with a single nation or national idea. But it does pull the rug from under any would-be multinational or supranational state, such as Austria-Hungary or the Soviet Union or the Socialist Federated Republic of Yugoslavia.

If the nation-state is the ideal (perhaps the only, according to some people, legitimate) political form, then the defense of the nation-state's sovereignty and independence becomes the national community's supreme moral duty, as argued by British neo-Hegelian philosopher Bernard Bosanquet (1848–1923). Moreover, as Bosanquet further explains, "the body which is to be in sole or supreme command of force for the common good must possess a true general will, and for that reason must be a genuine community sharing a common sentiment and animated by a common tradition."[6] This, in turn, suggests a collective right to national homogeneity—a point to which I return.

Further, advocacy of a right of national self-determination has been closely associated with the defense of a right of national secession—a recourse considered necessary to instrumentalize the achievement of near-homogeneous nation-states.

Myth 2: So-called political realism. The underlying premise of realism, whether in the classic Morgenthau tradition, in a Marxist guise, or attired in the garments of rational choice theory, is that interests should serve and do in fact serve as the guiding beacon of political action[7]—in effect identifying the real with the rational, as Hegel put it. But whereas Hegel, had he spoken the language of "interests," would have identified those interests with morality,[8] in effect acknowledging the reality of ethical interests, would-be realists think not of ethical interests but of national interests, economic self-interest, and, in some contexts, the political interests of officeholders, thereby reducing interests to power in its sundry forms,[9] with the result that the augmentation of power becomes its own purpose. It was, thus, purely in the realist tradition that, in June 1998, top officials at the Pentagon expressed their skepticism about any use of military force to stop Milošević's atrocities against the Albanian civilian population of Kosovo by urging that "Washington has no compelling national security interest in Kosovo," not even acknowledging that there might be compelling ethical interests (and duties) at stake.[10]

Hobbes's writings sowed many of the seeds that have sprouted as contemporary realism. Although Hobbes acknowledged the existence of Natural Law, he did not view the political order as serving any moral purpose, as most of his contemporaries did, but as serving the purposes of peace and security above all. Hence, in *De Cive* (1642), he urged that "*just* and *unjust* did not exist until commands were given; hence their nature is relative to a command; and every action in its own nature is indifferent. What is *just* or *unjust* derives from the right of the ruler."[11]

Realists often stress conflict as a constant in human history, and they are often seen as being pessimistic about human nature.[12] Conflict is explained as taking place variously between states, classes, or nations. However it may be construed, the conclusion is always the same: winning is preferable to losing. It is hard to imagine anyone arguing the reverse. But what if the nature of the essential value to be won or lost were grotesquely distorted? And what if, to take a second point, there might be an escape from conflict (or, at least, a means of reducing the frequency and ferocity of conflict)? Marx fantasized about such an escape, which he expected to result from the social, economic, ethnic, and religious (or rather, areligious) homogenization of the planet. Less fantastically, Kant argued that conflict could be reduced by erecting an international legal order that would regulate relations between states through the universalization of the rule of law (in effect, anticipating Wilsonianism in some ways, as well as some of the concepts underpinning the United Nations and the Council of Europe).[13] Kant denied, in the *Metaphysics of Morals*, that perpetual peace was achievable but insisted, all the same, that "the political principles directed toward perpetual peace, of entering into such alliances of states, which serve for continual *approximation* to it, are not unachievable."[14] In Kant's view, "war is the greatest of evils"[15]—the most potent vehicle for the radical evil that lies, in Kant's view, at the heart of human nature.[16]

What, then, is the realist myth? At base, realists affirm that states may serve their own short-term and long-term interests by building power, even if in this pursuit they do damage to human rights or justice or Natural Law or the general good. Idealists dispute this and urge, on the contrary, the centrality of these values to interests. Idealists hold that disregard for these loftier values risks undermining the very stability upon which self-declared realists ardently depend.

Myth 3: Value-free science as total freedom. Political realism, as noted above, already entails ethical neutrality, thereby revealing its organic connection with at least one understanding of value-free science. Morgenthau put it this way: "Realism maintains that universal moral principles cannot be applied to the actions of states in their abstract universal formulation, but that they must be filtered through the concrete circumstances of time and place."[17] Or, more precisely, they must—in the view of realists—be filtered through a consideration of the interests at stake for the relevant actors. Interests, not principles, shall rule in the community of nations. And, on this view, as Machiavelli once said, the greatest crime a prince might commit is not to advance the material interests of his state. The myth of a truly value-free science imports this amoral pursuit of interests into the world of science. Insofar as certain scientists may recognize no ethical boundaries in choice of object (e.g., cloning, genetic splicing, euthanasia), in scope of experimentation (e.g., use of animals as subjects when chemical testing can achieve the same result), or in application (e.g., Nazi science),[18] they proclaim the self-centered "total freedom" of Machiavelli or even Stirner, not the limited "ethical freedom" of Kant.

The notion of value-free science opens the door, in effect, to the incorporation of the moral relativism of political realism into its epistemology and methodology. In its incunabulum, the notion of value-free science was, however, healthy and essential, urging that one bring objectivity into one's methodology and not permit oneself to be guided by preferences derived from religious, ethnic, racial, cultural, financial, or other sources in framing the analytical problem and developing a research strategy. Had social scientists been willing to leave it at that, remaining content with the modest cast given to the notion by most hard scientists, it would be difficult to quarrel with it. Fortunately, many social scientists have remained content with that. But there has always been a temptation for some to embrace a full-blooded Machiavellian methodology, come what may. Under the impact of the War of Yugoslav Succession (1991–95), in particular, some social scientists even sought to impose a stricture, forbidding other social scientists to assess culpability in a war situation; rather, we were urged to consider it scientific to proceed from the a priori assumption that "all are guilty," building supposedly scientific conclusions on the rigid foundation of this relativistic doctrine.

The advocacy of such a notion of value-free science—which is to say, a science reluctant to distinguish good from evil—is, as Carol Lilly has noted, wedded to "amoral realism,"[19] and, as this relativizing argument makes clear, vital to the defense of the rights of nations against criticism rooted in moral outrage; that such advocacy may also serve to obstruct the assignment of primary guilt to one or another side in the War of Yugoslav Succession should be clear enough.

The notion of value-free science is generally thought to be useful in guarding the investigator against prejudices, preformed conclusions, distorted investigation, and what is conventionally called "normative bias," and, if understood in its original sense, it can serve these functions well. The value-free scientist is supposed to set upon his or her tasks without having a preferred outcome and, more significant, without allowing normative considerations to guide the selection of problems to be investigated. But there have, from time to time, been overenthusiastic practitioners of "value-free science," such as Nazi scientists who took on the assignment to develop new technology so that more Jews and Gypsies could be gassed at once. For enthusiasts, all themes and all subjects are equally deserving of investigation, regardless of social consequences, while the expression of horror at the consequences is somehow seen as a betrayal of one's scientific integrity.

THE PROBLEMS WITH NATIONALIST REALISM AND AMORAL SCIENCE

The values of "value-free" science. The notion that social science must be "value-free" to the point of declining to acknowledge guilt or even to "call a spade a spade" is based on a flawed historiography and on blatant self-contradiction. Historiographically, the modern science of international politics germinated in normative values. As E. H. Carr reminds us,

> The teleological aspect of the science of international politics has been conspicuous from the outset. It took its rise from a great and disastrous war; and the overwhelming purpose which dominated and inspired the pioneers of the new science was to obviate a recurrence of this disease of the international body politic. The passionate desire to prevent war determined the whole initial course and direction of the study.[20]

Moreover, the notion that science is truly value-free, if taken literally and to the extreme that some would like, reduces science to the arbitrary and erratic pursuit of knowledge for its own sake and without regard to utility. When medical researchers study cancer in humans, rather than the diseases that afflict the common house fly, it is because they value human life more than the lives of flies. Nor is it any use to refer this argument to interest, because the realist concept of interest presumes that interests are permanently in conflict—that is, that there might be persons, for example, whose interests would be better served by obstructing progress toward the treatment of cancer, and that a history of medical research might be interpreted as a struggle between these two conflicting interests.

In actual fact, all science is informed by values—whether the value of human health, or that of protecting the environment, or that of extending the horizons for direct travel—and values affect not only the choice of object of study but also the scope of the study, the methodology, and the applications sought. A Stirnerite political science purged of values would end up looking like a social science counterpart to "Nazi science," embracing a relativistic worldview holding "that 'right' means (can only be coherently understood as meaning) 'right for a given society'; that 'right for a given society' is to be understood in a functionalist sense; and that (therefore) it is wrong for people in one society to condemn, interfere with, etc., the values of another society"[21]—and, by extension, holding also that it is wrong for one scientist to criticize the values or purposes or another scientist unless, presumably, the latter is actually breaking the laws of the land. Nor is it clear how a social science purged of values might retain an interest in the vigor of tolerance in a given society, as Lilly warned,[22] even though, as Joseph Raz points out, tolerance has a good claim to being the single most important value to deserve protection, according to classical liberal thinking.[23]

Why realism is unrealistic. Machiavelli and Hobbes are variously credited with having been the *Urväter* of political realism, but, where Machiavelli is concerned, this claim is only partially accurate. For, unlike modern-day (or perhaps postmodern-day) realists, Machiavelli emphasized the necessity of appearing both moral and benevolent. In so urging, he recognized the existence of a universal moral law; he merely felt that sovereigns sometimes needed to ignore it. Contemporary realist writings do not necessarily share these suppositions.

The realist–idealist debate can be reduced to three core disputes, concerning the place of morally informed vision in policymaking, the feasibility of emphasizing and promoting the common interests of all parties to a given conflict, and the nature of interests themselves.

To take up the first two points together: contemporary realists have tended to urge policymakers to advance the immediate material and short-term security interests of their own state or states rather than the shared interests of an entire region (incidentally, urging policies based on a specific set of values and ethical dispositions rather than on the kind of purged science they profess to practise). The behavior of Clemenceau and Lloyd-George at Versailles, like that of Carrington, Owen, Hurd, and Major during the War of Yugoslav Succession, was classically realist in seeking to advance or protect the specific interests of Britain (in Clemenceau's case, France) and showed little real concern for the merits of the case on the ground. Whether there should have been plebiscites conducted after World War I in the South Tirol or in Transylvania or in what became southern Slovakia, or whether unity or separation of the nations of Bosnia (in 1991–95) according to one formula or another best accorded with the interests of the people constituting those nations, were not issues into which these politicians cared to enter. The reason is that they allowed themselves to be guided by the hope of safeguarding British or French interests, in effect subscribing to political realism in its classical mode. Their approach tended to emphasize the conflict of interests locally (between Germans and Poles, Hungarians and Romanians, Serbs and Muslims, etc.) rather than to identify common interests such as, in the Bosnian case, the reduction of xenophobia on all sides and the removal of those who were stoking up chauvinistic nationalism on all sides.

But to expect realists to concern themselves with common interests is to expect realists to think like idealists. Realists cannot be expected to concern themselves in the first place with achieving a just solution, much less with promoting justice in a peace settlement, in a region, or even in the world, justice being the quality inhering in legitimate government and not in one or another territorial settlement. For such realists, politics is a zero-sum game in which there are winners and losers: the whole notion of justice, in which all persons and groups are to some extent winners, is entirely foreign to pure realism.

Moreover, realists have been limited by an oversimplified view of interests (the third point registered above). Rather than allow, as John Spanier does, that a nation may have interests of an ethical or normative nature,[24] the realist antipathy between values and interests tends to emphasize the direct "material" interests of one nation versus another, be these interests economic, territorial, or matters of security or resources. For the realist, the only reason one agent may rationally support another's claim is in the hope of direct reciprocation on a matter considered important by that agent, or on the basis of an agreed price. Alan Gewirth counsels against such approach:

> The rational agent's recognition and support of other persons' positive rights does not have as its ground merely, or even primarily, a kind of "rational," strategic, self-centered calculation of how according these rights to others may probably help him to receive such help himself. The ground is primarily not one of reciprocity but rather of mutuality. It is not a contingent matter of quid pro quo but a necessary [a priori] matter of persons' common humanity as purposive agents. The agent recognizes that other persons are similar to her in being prospective purposive agents and having the needs of agency, and on this ground she rationally accepts that they have the same positive rights she necessarily claims for herself. Thus a kind of community, a common status of having needs that require for their fulfillment the positive help of others, lies in the background of the argument for positive rights, so that rights and community are in this way also brought together.[25]

But if, as Spanier implies and as Kant explicitly urges, the interests of justice, toleration, and freedom cannot be divorced from the "material" interests of states, then the endeavor to sacrifice the former in order to achieve the latter can only founder and end in disaster. The fundamental premises of political realism, in a word, are utterly unrealistic and, if blindly followed, can only be unrealistic. "Idealists," in spite of the sarcastic way many use the term, are more truly realistic, in urging that peace, prosperity, and harmony among nations can be fostered only by promoting the values upon which they are founded. Kant would have agreed with Machiavelli on the importance that any peace settlement appear to be just; but where Kant departs from Machiavelli is in his conviction that the reality of justice is also essential.

The Great Powers' leaders have, with a very few exceptions— Woodrow Wilson, Franklin Delano Roosevelt, and Jimmy Carter come to mind—operated on the basis of political realism. Pure realists are even vulnerable to criticism on the basis of their own values. The results speak for themselves. The Treaty of Berlin, signed in 1878, was supposed to serve the interests of Britain and France by reducing the territorial extent of Bulgaria (expected to remain a protégé of Russia, a future British and French ally) and the interests of Austria-Hungary by assigning control of the Ottoman province of Bosnia-Herzegovina (albeit, shorn of Novi Pazar) to it. In actual fact, this product of the realist school sowed deep animosities in Bulgaria, opened Macedonia to fierce competition among Serbia, Bulgaria, and Greece, destabilized much of the region, and politicized Bosnia's Muslims—thereby setting the stage for the Balkan Wars of 1912–13 and World War I. To claim that this realist-motivated diplomacy was, in fact, realistic, one would have to believe that both long-term Balkan instability and the outbreak of continent-wide warfare in 1914, in the course of which both Britain and France suffered enormous demographic and economic losses, served the interests of those two powers. This seems a dubious proposition. The alternative is to suggest that disregarding the wishes of locals, as Britain and France did, was ill conceived and not at all realistic either in the short term or in the long term.

So-called realism triumphed again at the London Conference in 1913, which recognized Albania within truncated borders and legitimated the Serbian conquest of a large chunk of the newly declared state, even though the local majority was Albanian and preferred union with Albania, thereby unnecessarily stoking resentment and discontent and sowing the seeds of future instability. Britain and France wanted to keep Albania small because of Albania's friendship with Austria-Hungary. Neither peace nor stability was of much concern to the British and French diplomats at the conference, however. But the problems created by the assignment of Kosovo to Serbia have continued to this day, playing a not inconsiderable role in the destabilization of socialist Yugoslavia and occasioning NATO's first war.

Realism and idealism clashed at the Paris peace talks of 1919–20, embodied respectively in the figures of Clemenceau and Wilson. But, with the exception of the establishment of the League of Nations, the provisions of the treaties were inspired more by the self-serving avarice associated with Clemenceau's brand of realism than with the "mutuality of needs"

(Gewirth's phrase) associated with idealism. Whether one speaks of the punitive reparations imposed on Germany by the Allies; or the confiscation of Germany's overseas colonies by Britain, France, and Japan (rather than their liberation); or the highly selective use of plebiscites (holding them in Schleswig-Holstein, Silesia, and Burgenland but not in Alsace-Lorraine, southern Slovakia, Vojvodina, Transylvania, Sudetenland, Kosovo, western Prussia, or Südtirol where Allied preferences were likely to be rejected by locals, all the while singing the praises of national self-determination)—in all of these cases, interest-driven realism guided the treaties' framers.

I would deny that there is any blanket right of national self-determination that would justify the breakup of legitimate states or the arbitrary action of irredentist groups. But when an empire collapses, someone has to establish the borders of the new states that emerge out of its political cadaver. This could be diplomats from the Great Powers sitting in Paris or in some other city, or it could be those living in the area themselves, that is, those who will be most directly affected. In such circumstances, the only legitimate basis for drawing new borders in the contemporary age—I would suggest—is through a plebiscite among local residents, recognizing not a right of national self-determination but a conditional right of local self-determination, operative in conditions of system collapse.

In fact, the peace settlements after World War I, in which the winners gorged themselves on the colonies of the defeated powers and the losers were stripped of land (Germany and Bulgaria) or chopped up into a number of states (Austria-Hungary, the Ottoman Empire), proved to be untenable, provoking desires for vengeance and territorial revision in the affected states, and ultimately dangerous for all of Europe, including those states whose diplomats thought they were benefitting from the arrangements concluded in Paris. Had the sundry peace treaties drafted in Paris been prepared with an eye to justice and the mutuality of needs, it is arguable, à la A. J. P. Taylor, that there would have been no Third Reich, no Holocaust, and no World War II.[26] On this argument, to defend the foreign policy realism of Versailles in a consistent and comprehensive way, one would have to argue that the Third Reich, the Holocaust, and the savagery of World War II were all in the best interests of Britain and France at least, if not of the other victorious Great Powers as well. Such an argument should strike all except neo-Nazis as implausible.

Arguments derived from the mutuality of needs and from the importance of fairness and justice suggest that the repudiation of values results, over the long term, in injury to one's own material interests. In consequence, only idealism serves the long-term interests (including material interests) or powers; political realism is a shortcut to disaster. Realism is unrealistic.

WHY THERE ARE NO NATIONAL RIGHTS

I alluded, in the foregoing section, to certain counterproductive territorial arrangements made in Berlin, London, and Paris over the years 1878–1920. It is not by accident that I nowhere refer to the right of national self-determination as a principle being violated. I alluded to instability, local discontent, resentment, and the inability to move forward with democratization as unfortunate results of certain ill-conceived treaties. To my mind, however, the denial of national self-determination entails no self-contradiction, if only because I do not believe that there is any such right. This is not to justify land grabs by greedy powers; it is, on the contrary, a plea for working within existing borders, where they are geostrategically and economically viable, and for prioritizing the human rights of people over the claims registered on behalf of national groups.

On this point, my own thinking is close to Kant's, albeit by analogy. In discussing his belief that there is no right of rebellion, Kant insists quite consistently that people must obey whatever sovereign exercises authority in their land. Thus, although no revolution or rebellion can ever legitimately claim the allegiance of the people against the established government, "once a revolution has succeeded and a new constitution has been established, the lack of legitimacy with which it began and has been implemented cannot release the subjects from the obligation to comply with the new order of things as good citizens, and they cannot refuse honest obedience to the [new] authority that now has the power."[27]

By the same virtue, I would argue that there is no nationally derived natural right of secession, but should such a secession succeed, its success would generate neither a right for further secessions from the new state nor a right to resort to arms to restore the original union. War and violence, as Kant notes, can never (or rather, almost never, in my own view) be legitimately launched; or, to put it differently, there can never be a right to insurrection or to a war of aggression. (The sole qualification to this maxim is insurrection to overthrow or escape from tyranny—for reasons to be discussed in the final section of this chapter.)

The claim to a universal right of national self-determination, like claims by nationalists that there is a right to government subsidies for the cultural and social organizations of one or another nationality group, must be situated within the theory of rights more generally. Legal philosophy admits of only three kinds of rights: divine rights, natural rights, and positive rights.[28] That national self-determination or the claim on government monies could be a divine right may be dismissed at once on the grounds that no major religion includes either of these alleged rights among its doctrines, that no references to such rights are found in the scriptures of any known religion, that the wishes of a supposed supreme deity concerning border questions or government funding cannot be readily ascertained or documented, and that the very existence (not to mention, nature) of such a being (or group of beings) remains a matter of dispute. Nor is it admissible to assert that national self-determination and the claim on government monies are positive rights, since the exercise of such a right must, by definition, depend on the laws passed by the state in question, and to claim that there is a positive right against positive laws is to embrangle oneself in self-contradiction. Moreover, there is no international convention granting a blanket positive right of self-determination to all self-declared national groups; indeed, it is hardly likely that a proposition to such an effect could garner much support. Thus, it appears that to claim a universal positive right of national self-determination would be to claim that all[29] states actually do permit the secession of their territorial parts, when inhabited by people who claim to have a distinct nationality or language—a claim that would be patently false. As a result, when people claim that there are rights of national self-determination or rights of national groups (ethnic associations) to claim funds for cultural or social activities in which they wish to indulge, these claims can be seriously mounted only on the supposition of natural right, which is to say on the basis of a right grounded in Natural Law.

The alleged natural right of ethnic associations to government funding. Let us consider first the claim that ethnic associations have a natural right to government funding for their activities. Natural Law is the moral law and has no specific national content. If the claim is that any national group has a claim on government funding, then this claim may be sustained only if *any* group, regardless of its purpose and activities, can register a claim to the same level of funding as long as it is not operating in violation of the law. Thus, the mafia, human traffickers, terrorists, and groups involved in political assassinations could not lay claim to government funding even if such a general right were conceded. But if our well-meaning nationalists are to have their way, then every philatelic club, yodeling club, rock star fan club, séance society, ventriloquists' association, and academic association would have to be granted equal claims on government funding and, in the absence of some other measure to which a majority of citizens would give their assent, on the basis of funding proportional to membership (so that a ventriloquists' association with twice the membership of an ethnic association would receive twice the funding). The assertion of such a right could end up being rather costly, and citizens of Eastern Europe, never mind the United States, are unlikely to be enthusiastic about bankrolling the activities of every association or club that pops up.

What is my objection to the funding of ethnic associations? I do not object to government funding of such associations as may be deemed (via democratic procedures) worthy of support; if ethnic associations are deemed worthy of support, then so be it. Nor am I an advocate of cultural homogenization; on the contrary, I have always been convinced that a society is richer if its members can preserve their cultural heritage, and that preservation is, generally speaking, preferable to amnesia. My objection is to the philosophically insupportable notion that associations of any kind can ground a claim to government funding in Natural Law. Such a claim reflects, to my mind, a grotesque ignorance of Natural Law and/or a willingness to make claims without even thinking through the ramifications of the claims being advanced.

The alleged natural right of national self-determination. The first difficulty confronting secessionist-minded nationalists is that nationalism is, of its essence, morally relativistic rather than morally universalistic.[30] A nationalist does not talk about what is good for the human community, still less of what is good for all species, but about what is good for his or her nation. A nationalist seeks to prioritize the interests of his or her own nation and cannot pay equal attention to the interests of other nations without ceasing to be a nationalist. As such, nationalism stands in tension with, if not overtly repudiating, Natural Law. By denying Natural Law, the nationalist denies the only possible ground for the presumed right he or she wishes to enjoy and ends up with no basis for asserting natural rights. Moral consequentialism, moral conventionalism, and moral contractarianism all entail a denial of the existence of natural rights,[31] and therefore these approaches (and, in bastardized form, consequentialism in particular) constitute precisely the moral foundations of nationalism.

The second difficulty is that, even if our would-be nationalist offers to embrace moral universalism (which holds that all people of all races and nations are of equal moral worth, enjoy the same natural rights, and ought to enjoy the same positive rights), how is she or he to deal with the circumstances that Natural Law theory derives all rights from duties, that rights are thought to be linked to corresponding duties? To put it another way, if a national group enjoys the right to secede, the state must have a duty to permit that group to secede, and if any self-declared group has the right to secede, then the state must be seen to have a duty to allow any group of persons wishing to secede to do so, provided only that they declare that they constitute a nationally unique group. But, perhaps ironically, nationalists rarely, if ever, make the latter claim. Moreover, if the nation-state is the ideal, then the dominant national group within the given state must be entitled to define which language or languages will be official and what will be the content of officially permitted culture—a claim registered, in fact, by Francisco Franco in Spain when he forbade the use of the Catalan language in public, by Nicolae Ceaușescu in Romania when he endeavored to suppress the Hungarian culture among Hungarians who had been forcibly incorporated into Romania after World War I, among others. And if Franco and Ceaușescu are thought to have been entitled to take such actions, then it would follow—for such persons who might be latter-day supporters of past authoritarian regimes—that the Catalans and Hungarians had a duty—the word sticks in the throat—to relinquish their indigenous languages and cultures upon demand. Yet this proposition entails self-contradiction since the same group is seen by the nationalist to be both entitled to secede and duty-bound to relinquish culture and language, depending only, apparently, on the ethnicity of the nationalist in question and of the group specified. Moreover, it lands the nationalist in the twilight realm of pure subjectivity not far from the pseudo-metaphysics of Max Stirner. Nationalists, it seems, affirm and deny the same maxim in the same breath.

But there is a third difficulty, namely, that the doctrine of national self-determination directly contradicts an essential corollary of moral universalism: "Any action is *right* if it can coexist with everyone's freedom in accordance with a universal law, or if on its maxim the freedom of choice of each can coexist with everyone's freedom in accordance with a universal law."[32] In other words, the exercise of such a right (of national self-determination) *always* violates the rights of others, regardless of their number. Even if the support for secession within subregion X of the Republic of Z were 100%, that secession would violate the rights of those citizens remaining within rump-Z (except, as already mentioned, in the case of Z being ruled by a tyrant). Or, to put it another way, moral universalism does not legitimate the exercise of a right of national self-determination, and if a "right" may never be exercised, then it is not a right at all. This argument is not so different from that of James Madison in the *Federalist Papers,* or from that of John Stuart Mill in *On Liberty.* In *Federalist Paper* No. 51, specifically,

Madison is concerned to prevent majority rule from threatening the rights of a minority, however defined, and Mill *begins* his 1859 tract with a warning about "the tyranny of the majority [which] is now generally included among the evils against which society requires us to be on its guard."[33]

There is yet a fourth difficulty with this doctrine. If there were a right of national self-determination, it would, of necessity, take the form of "all Serbs have the right to live in one state," as Dobrica Ćosić and Slobodan Milošević put it in the 1990s, because, if the claim were construed rather as "some Serbs have the right to live in one state," then the state would be premised on an inequality of rights among coethnics, which is to say on a right that is sometimes enjoyed, sometimes not. But if the nationalists' alleged right to have a state of their own is granted, that would entail a further claim that "Serbs have a right to live by themselves," since, if this right is omitted, inevitably the "national right" of one or another group would be violated. In other words, the assertion of a right of national self-determination entails a legitimation of "ethnic cleansing" (which is to say, of genocide, as it is defined in the U.N.'s Genocide Convention).

Why should this be so? Let us imagine that we have a nation known as Aybecedia, in which Aybecedians are intermixed with Jaykayellians, and that the Aybecedians are in the majority. Let us suppose, further, that Aybecedia consists of five provinces with the following population distribution:

Province A: 2,100,000 *Aybecedians,*   0 *Jaykayellians*
Province B: 3,200,000 *Aybecedians,*   2,000 *Jaykayellians*
Province C: 2,450,000 *Aybecedians,*   0 *Jaykayellians*
Province D: 1,800,000 *Aybecedians,*   370,000 *Jaykayellians*
Province E: 1,950,000 *Aybecedians,*   1,200,000 *Jaykayellians*

And let us further suppose that the Aybecedians are so intermixed with the Jaykayellians in provinces B, D, and E that it would be utterly impossible to draw any border without leaving some of each group within the territory controlled by the other. In other words, imagine a territory bearing, in this regard, some resemblance to Bosnia-Herzegovina in 1991, where three groups—Serbs, Croats, and Muslims/Bosniaks—were intermixed. It is immediately apparent that unless our Jaykayellians wished to change their status from being a minority in one Aybecedian-dominated state to being a minority in two Aybecedian-dominated states, the only recourse they could have in the endeavor to exercise their supposed right of national self-determination (thereby asserting their supposed right to determine the official language(s) of the state and define its culture) would be either to reduce the Aybecedians to second-class status (the Ruandan model) or to expel most or all of the Aybecedians from those districts in which they intended to create their state. Thus, there can be no right of national self-determination without either at least a contingent right to practise ethnic and cultural discrimination or a right of ethnic cleansing, that is, a right to perpetrate genocide.

It should be recalled that doctrine advocates are seeking to reconcile their claims with Natural Law and that the central principle of Natural Law is the maxim, "I ought never to act except in such a way that I can also will that my maxim should become a universal law."[34] Kant restates this rule in the *Metaphysics of Morals,* adding the crucial corollary, "Any maxim [or act] that does not so qualify is contrary to morals."[35] Unless one can claim that the world would be a better place if people everywhere practiced discrimination as they saw fit, or if they killed off those whose presence they found inconvenient if they deemed it appropriate, one cannot feel legitimated in claiming genocide as a natural right; moreover, anyone seriously making such a claim could only be judged completely insane. It appears that Natural Law can never legitimate the taking of life, as entailed in the claim to a right of "ethnic cleansing," thus demonstrating that the doctrine of a right of national self-determination stands in direct contradiction to Natural Law.

This objection may be raised to the foregoing argument: the claim that all coethnics should live in one state needs to be qualified with reference to existing boundaries. Accordingly, Serbia had a right to go it alone, just as Croatia did, but it did not have a right to take Croatia's Serbs (or even Bosnia's Serbs) with it. But this transparent effort to salvage the "right" by tying it to the doctrine of *uti possidetis*[36] is doomed to fail, because these are contrary principles, not complementary ones. If the right of self-determination abides in the entire people living in a given state community (or in their government), then it is not a national right at all but a state right.

Further possible objections. It might be argued that, in associating the doctrine of the right of national self-determination with political realism, even if I do not equate them, I am forgetting that Woodrow Wilson, perhaps the doctrine's greatest champion in the twentieth century, was the quintessential idealist, and that Herder himself was a romantic nationalist, not a classical realist. Is this a case of conflating realism with idealism—or more, of outright misattribution? That the national doctrine and the realist school enjoyed separate births is clear enough, but they have become associated over time. Already in the nineteenth century, diplomats of the Great Powers did not hesitate to mouth the rhetoric of self-determination while seeking to advance their own material and security interests. More particularly, in the course of the nineteenth century, nationalism became the legitimating cover for the pursuit of the state's material interests, and the appearance of honoring the supposed national rights of smaller nations served, in turn, to present one's own state as gracious and noble, even while providing legitimation for the ideology of nationalism. In the past century, moreover, despite their different births, both have become part of the common stock of mainstream political thinking.

It might also be argued that rights are ultimately subjective, that rights are what people think they are (the position of pure nominalists). The corollary is that if people think they enjoy a certain right, then, by virtue of their belief alone, they come into possession of that right. Such solipsistic argumentation might be acceptable on conventionalist grounds, but quite apart from the philosophical limitations and moral relativism of conventionalism,[37] a right can only be understood—as Mary Gregor notes, summarizing Kant—as "a capacity to put another under obligation."[38] In other words, the notion of rights presumes that there is consensus about rights (as is implied in the concept of Universal Reason). Elsewhere, in the *Doctrine of Right,* Kant defines his subject as "the sum of laws for which an external lawgiving is possible,"[39] thus linking right with obligation via their connection in (natural or positive) law.

A possible third objection would hold that the democratic principle provides that people may claim the right to associate with whichever state they choose, to secede from one state, to set up independent republics at will, even to seek to have the territory in which they live annexed to a neighboring state. But nationalists seeking to found their claims on democratic theory are obliged to demonstrate why nationality, rather than religion or some other shared trait should enjoy primacy in establishing the legitimacy of state borders or, for that matter, why a shared trait authorizes a group to terminate its association with others not sharing this trait. Until doctrine advocates accomplish that task, why should skeptics give greater credence to a supposed right of national self-determination than to equivalent principles declared on the basis of religion, social class, political orientation, or cultural compatibility? Moreover, doctrine advocates need to resolve the dilemma set by the fact that the consistent exercise of this supposed right would result in indefinite secessions, subsecessions, and subsubsecessions—and, further, that the existence of ethnically mixed areas poses a problem soluble *only* by ignoring the human rights of persons living in those areas and by repudiating Natural Law altogether.

TOWARD A THEORY OF RIGHTS

The preceding argument concerning claims to national rights was to some extent presaged in a debate published in *Political Theory* in 1992 between two thoughtful students of nationalities affairs, Chandran Kukathas and Will Kymlicka. In the course of two articles for that journal, Kukathas outlined a position close to my own. Kymlicka, in a reply to the first of these, presented an articulate case for the contrary view.[40] What is, I think, distinctive in the present chapter is the endeavor to harness Natural Law theory explicitly to the analysis of the question at hand.

St. Thomas Aquinas (ca. 1225–74), although not the originator of the concept of Natural Law (which was already common currency in Cicero's time), gave this concept its first systematic and comprehensive expostulation. Linking this law with what the Stoics had called "immanent reason" (and which I have called Universal Reason),[41] Aquinas explained:

> Now among all others the rational creature is subject to Divine providence in the most excellent way, in so far as it partakes of a share of providence, by being provident both for itself and for others. Wherefore it has a share of the Eternal Reason, whereby it has a natural inclination to its proper act and end: and this participation of the eternal law in the rational creat[ur]e is called the natural law.[42]

Kant's teaching on Natural Law added to that of Aquinas in two important respects. First, like Hobbes,[43] Kant dismissed the notion that God's will could serve as the ultimate foundation of morality, tracing the moral sense to universally shared reason.[44] Second, having rejected all heteronomous sources of morality, Kant declared that moral concepts can arise only a priori, and never a posteriori—that is, moral principles "cannot be abstracted from any empirical, and therefore merely contingent, knowledge."[45] In so saying, Kant attributed to reason a higher degree of certainty than Aquinas had conceded.

Earlier in this chapter, I argued that advocates of the doctrine of national self-determination are unable to establish the status of the supposed national right because, in several important regards, it is incompatible with Natural Law, the source of all natural rights. It is, however, important to stress that both individual and societal rights are protected under Natural

Law, because they are firmly embedded in interlocking networks of duties. *Individual rights* include the right to preserve one's life, to own property, to develop one's faculties, to hold such religious and philosophical views as one judges appropriate, to speak one's mind (as long as no injury is intended thereby), and to associate with those from whose company or shared interests one derives satisfaction. What I call *societal rights* include rights enjoyed not by individuals qua individuals, but communally. These include a society's right to public security, to a functioning public education system, to low-cost medical care, to the commitment of the state to uphold a system of justice broadly compatible with Natural Law, and the like.[46] Society's rights entail corresponding duties on the part of the state, just as the rights of individuals entail corresponding duties (if only of respect for them) on the part of other individuals as well as of the state. As I have noted elsewhere, some of those rights that are claimed as "national rights" are in fact individual rights shared by a group of people. As individuals, they are entitled to aggregate for the pursuit of shared goals and interests. Natural rights of this order would include

> the right to obtain education in one's own language, where there are enough students with that native language to warrant classes; the right to develop and pursue one's own culture, together with fellow members of that culture (including converts); [and] the right to establish cultural and educational institutions funded from private funds or from funds generated by the members of that community.[47]

My argument, thus, is not that national groups do not have rights. On the contrary, they enjoy all those rights based on the aggregation of the individual rights of their members and all those societal rights in which they partake as sectors of a broader society. What I am denying is, rather, that there are specific "national rights," such as alleged rights to secession, to ethnic autonomy, to cultural hegemonism (suppressing the languages and cultures of local minorities), to mass murder and cultural annihilation dressed up as "cleansing," to confiscation of the houses and property of members of another nation,[48] or to state funding for the cultural institutions, radio stations, newspapers, and ethnic events of specific nationality groups (unless such funding is specifically guaranteed under positive law in the given state or negotiated among the relevant partners). To the extent that one wished to establish a modified right of national self-determination at a lower level, one would have to derive it from clearly recognized individual rights. Thus, for

example, individuals are generally recognized to enjoy a natural right to em-
igrate, provided that they meet the legal requirements of both countries affected. From this, one may legitimately derive a collective (or "national")
right of emigration, assuming only that no laws are broken and all legal requirements met. But just as an individual does not enjoy a right to declare
her house sovereign or to declare it to be under the sovereignty or protection of a foreign power,[49] so too, nations taking leave of a given state are not
entitled to take their land with them—with one exception.

That exception, to which I have already alluded at least twice, is the
right (and duty) to oppose tyranny. This exception was first established, not
by Kant, but by John Locke, and it centers on the question of tyranny. If we
define tyranny—as the medievals did[50]—as the comprehensive departure
on the part of the sovereign from the canons of Natural Law, then, in conditions of tyranny, sovereignty is temporarily vested in the people, who are
not only authorized, but indeed duty-bound, to overthrow the tyrannical
government and to appoint another in better harmony with the moral law
and better suited to realizing the purposes for which government is established, to paraphrase Locke. Locke was writing in justification of the exclusion of James II from the throne of England; hence, his defense of popular
sovereignty was an essential element in his advocacy of what amounted to
Whig revolution. But the same principle could be cited in justification of the
declarations of independence by Slovenia and Croatia in 1991, since, if a society is unable to overthrow a tyrant, whatever the reason for that deficiency
may be, individual parts of that society are entitled to remove themselves
from that tyranny.

Now, it might be thought that the right to escape from tyranny lays the
theoretical foundation for a right of national self-determination. But, in fact,
such reasoning would be flawed—in the first place because the right to escape tyranny provides no grounds for aggregating right at the level of nation,
and in the second place, because advocates of secessionism (as the example
of Quebec makes clear) do not wish to be limited in the exercise of this option to clearly tyrannical situations. Moreover, if tyranny is a moral problem,
it is a problem for the entire people of the given state—even if other parts
of the society are not themselves subjected to tyrannical repression—and
not just for one or another national group. When the Serbian government
despoiled Kosovar Albanians of their individual human rights, thus, this
was a moral problem for all citizens of Serbia. To deny this is to embrace
moral hedonism, in which rights and duties both evanesce, leaving only
the license for self-gratification and self-interest. To put it another way, if

the concept of rights is to be protected in a given society, then the rights of all permanent residents must be protected equally.

CONCLUSION

The doctrine of the right of national self-determination has been pernicious in its effects. And let no one doubt but that the proclamation of this so-called right by Wilson and Lenin, and its widespread validation, including for that matter by sundry scholars,[51] has encouraged people to take up arms on behalf of the nation. Ideas are not without their effects, and bad ideas are apt to have bad effects. While no set of ideas can solve problems absolutely, the widespread abandonment of the doctrine of the right of national self-determination might well have a salutary and pacifying effect in certain troubled areas, removing at the same time at least one source of violations of human rights.[52] The question of tyranny, which constitutes the one exception to the proscription of secession, cannot be put to use in the service of this doctrine, which remains incompatible with the moral universalism of Natural Law.

As already noted in chapters 1 and 3, the societies of Eastern Europe can hope for long-term stability only to the extent that they develop and maintain legitimate systems. And legitimacy (the subject of chapter 2 and of the concluding chapter) in turn entails the harmonization of the sociopolitical-economic system with universal standards of morality, standards I subsume under the rubric of Natural Law.

6

THREE MODELS
OF CHURCH–STATE
CONDOMINIUM

Across post-communist Europe, a battle is being waged over the moral content of democracy. This is a battle over whether the religious market should be open or closed, over whether the dominant religious organization should be able to translate its moral convictions into laws binding on all citizens regardless of their religious affiliation, over the proper exercise and limits of freedom of speech, and even over the putative right of a religious body (whether the Catholic or the Orthodox Church) to harness the political apparatus in one or another state for the purpose of obtaining exceptions to EU standards. It is, in short, a battle over whether the dominant social system in post-communist Europe will be liberal democracy or clerical democracy.

By *liberal* democracy, we may understand a democratic system founded on the rule of law which protects and advances individual and societal rights and the values of tolerance, respect for the harm principle, and equality, and which is committed to the neutrality of the state in matters of religion. By *clerical* democracy, we may understand a democratic system founded on the principle that the content of positive law (secular law) should be in accord with divine law (as interpreted by the dominant religious association), which renders individual rights, claims to tolerance, and claims to equality relative to divine law, which reinterprets the harm principle in such a way as to actually prescribe or allow harm against those whose convictions or life-styles are not in accord with the moral agenda of the dominant religion, and which accordingly rejects state neutrality in matters of religion.

The signs of this struggle are everywhere to be seen—in the Russian Orthodox Church's success in 1997 in obtaining legislation which effectively choked off proselytism by foreign-based missionaries, in the Romanian Orthodox Church's frantic struggle to prevent the national parliament from decriminalizing homosexuality, and in the fight waged by both the Catholic and the Orthodox Church at the dawn of the present century over the constitution for the presumably secular EU (because those drafting that constitution did not consider it appropriate to mention God in the constitution's preamble).

This chapter reviews the politics of the Catholic Church in Poland, the Czech Republic, and Slovakia since 1989. Among other things, this chapter will consider debates concerning the constitutions and other legislation, the role of the church in national elections, controversies about abortion, homosexuality, and censorship, and the still unresolved question of property restitution in the Czech and Slovak republics.

Clerical democracy and liberal democracy may be understood as ideal types, in the Weberian sense, with concrete embodiments being closer to one or the other type. The three cases examined below represent a study in contrasts. Poland is, to a high degree, a clerical democracy, while the Czech Republic, by contrast, is closer to the ideal type of liberal democracy. In Slovakia, on the other hand, neither model is hegemonic, and a struggle continues between the advocates of clericalism and the champions of liberalism.

LIBERALISM AND CHRISTIAN RELIGION

As already seen in chapter 2, *liberalism* is taken here to mean a value system that places primacy on individual rights, toleration, human equality, and respect for the harm principle, among other things.[1] In conceptualizing liberalism in this way, I am construing liberalism as a moral orientation to be defended or undermined depending on the political formula which is adopted. Democracy, as a political formula, may assume a liberal or an illiberal form, and, in the latter form, may be at variance with one or more of the central liberal principles.

Historically, Christianity has been about truth. The Catholic and Orthodox Churches are not alone in having emphasized that truth cannot be submitted to debate or referendum,[2] that the church's interpretations of the moral law are binding and nonnegotiable, and that the church's authority trumps that of the secular state in matters of morality. Liberalism, by contrast, as John Stuart Mill forcefully argued in his *On Liberty,* is about the acceptance of the principle that minority opinions must be tolerated—indeed, that the opinions and views of the minority might turn out to be correct, and those of the majority, incorrect. Although liberalism has its "truths," these truths are procedural in nature, rather than doctrinal; liberalism does not dictate conclusions about policy (e.g., about whether to allow abortion or not) but rather the procedures for arriving at a decision and the expectations people may have about the process. Insofar as liberalism opens the door to religious tolerance, the secular state, neutral in matters of religion, is the logical instrument for assuring a modicum of social harmony founded not on unanimity about doctrine but on respect for the diversity of doctrines to which its populace may subscribe. *The Encyclopedia of Catholicism* notes that liberalism, "[r]ooted in the Enlightenment's belief in the free and scientific inquiry of individual persons, . . . has customarily provided a significant challenge to political and ecclesiastical authority."[3]

When I say that liberalism's "truths" are procedural in nature I mean that the core programmatic principles outlined in chapter 2—the rule of law, respect for individual rights and for the harm principle, equality, tolerance, and neutrality of the state in matters of religion—provide a framework for political life and for the resolution of issues in dispute. There are, of course, gray areas—famously, the question of abortion, referred to variously as the right of a woman to have an abortion and the right of a child not to be aborted. But the existence of gray areas, far from troubling us, should be reassuring, insofar as it reminds us that the duty to think through difficult problems cannot be wiped away simply by embracing a procedural formula.

But liberalism is more than just procedural in character; it also brings with it a moral framework, one linking the moral law with reason. Although St. Thomas Aquinas famously argued the case for reason-based Natural Law, he pointedly allowed that some matters could not be resolved through reason alone, appealing, in those instances, to Divine Law—in other words, the authority of the church. Today there are people who believe that morality is dependent upon the commands of a divine being—which assumes that reason is no guide at all—just as there are persons who tie morality to sentiment—the feeling of solidarity one may have for one's fellow human beings. Liberalism challenges both of these orientations by arguing that what is moral or immoral can normally be discerned by the exercise of reason and, by placing its stress exclusively on Natural Law (and thereby excluding Divine Law from consideration), also distinguishes its orientation from that of Aquinas.

If liberalism is to prevail in a given society, its values must be conveyed in the first place through education. Historically, religion has had a strong presence in the school systems of both Europe and the United States, and it is during the twentieth century that the concept of secular education has won strong support. Yet even today, there are those in the United States, for example, who want the public schools to teach a theory of "intelligent design" in place of evolution, in spite of the scientific establishment's unanimous endorsement of the theory of evolution. Or again, the posting of the Ten Commandments in American public schools or the hanging of crucifixes in classrooms in Bavaria serve notice that the advocates of these displays want to identify their schools as specifically Christian. Given that there are Muslims in Bavaria and people of diverse faiths in the United States, these moves serve notice on non-Christians that they are "outsiders," and that the schools are not fully theirs. In Poland and elsewhere, one can find schools teaching that homosexuality is "abnormal" and "wrong," thereby asserting the right of a society to veto an individual's choice of a life partner—perhaps the single most important right any individual is likely to demand.

CLERICAL DEMOCRACY— THE CASE OF POLAND

In Poland, the Roman Catholic Church has come into conflict with all six of the fundamental principles of liberalism. Where the rule of law is concerned, the church's insistence that ratification of the concordat be accomplished before passage of the constitution and the constitution adjusted to be compatible with the concordat,[4] rather than the reverse, was in itself an important symptom of the church's conviction that positive law must be subordinate to Natural Law and Divine Law. Indeed, in March 1997, the Constitutional Committee of the National Assembly ruled on precisely this question, finding that written law could *not* take precedence over Natural Law.[5] The church also successfully beat down an effort to put the question of abortion to a referendum, on the argument that Divine Law must be supreme—an argument at variance with the secular spirit of the rule of law. Moreover, as Adam Hetnal has noted, "[e]ven in the territories once dominated by non-Catholics, the Church has claimed and frequently received former religious property of other denominations"[6]—again, in contravention of customary understandings of the rule of law. Moreover, its campaign to insert the words "In the name of God" into the preamble to the constitution of Poland, like its demand that the EU constitution include an acknowledgment of Europe's Christian heritage, suggests that the church does not view either Poland or the EU as secular, but somehow as manifestations of the divine order. For the rule of law, this is a highly problematic interpretation.

Second, as has already been stressed above, the Catholic Church has asserted its putative entitlement to set the boundaries for individual rights. Thus, for the church, there is no right to a same-sex partner, no right to divorce, no right to an abortion (in the church's view, even when the mother's life is in danger), and no right to sex education except for pre-marriage education in which the obligation to raise one's children as practicing Catholics receives some stress. Even the decision whether or not to engage in premarital sex is removed from the individual's judgment and declared to be a matter for the authority of the church. The church's arrogation to itself of authority to set the boundaries of individual rights puts it squarely in conflict with liberalism.

The third functional minimal condition for liberalism—tolerance— was violated by the introduction of Catholic-only religious instruction in Poland's public schools, by barring academic discussions of homosexuality or transsexualism on Polish television or radio, and by the church's involvement with the homophobic League of Polish Families, among other things.

The church's insistence on maintaining the restrictive law on abortion in the face of statistics showing the risks to health posed by the illegal abortions which large numbers of Polish women now have as their only recourse, combined with the registered cases of babies dumped in the trash or in the river, suggests that the church has not found a solution which meets its own criteria of success. Further, the church's stand violates the harm principle, the fourth *Grundprinzip* of liberalism.

The fifth principle, equality, was violated by Polish prelates during the 1995 presidential race when they made hysterical attacks on Aleksander Kwaśniewski, the candidate of the Democratic Left Alliance (SLD), calling him a "neo-pagan" and castigating his party for allegedly nurturing an "anti-God complex."[7] Although church spokespersons have repeatedly declared that the church stays outside politics, prelates have continued to violate this self-declared principle. In the 2000 presidential elections, for example, the archbishop of Białystok advised Catholics that they "may not with a clear conscience vote for a candidate who is a supporter of abortion and demoralization."[8] The statement was directed against President Kwaś-niewski, who went on to win a second term as president of the republic.

And finally, the sixth principle, neutrality of the state in matters of religion, was from the beginning considered entirely illegitimate by the church. This was shown, inter alia, in the church's successful lobbying to have clauses inserted into a law on broadcasting which effectively barred any discussion of topics considered taboo by Poland's Catholic hierarchy. It was further demonstrated by the aforementioned introduction of Catholic religious instruction into the public schools (effective August 3, 1990) and the passage of the restrictive law on abortion in 1993.

More recently, the Catholic Church has vigorously criticized the EU constitution, most especially its preamble, demanding that Poland and other Catholic countries be given explicit guarantees against being pressured to legalize abortion. The Catholic Church has also warned that the EU's urging of countries to decriminalize homosexuality and institute legal protections for same-sex couples violates God's law and specifically threatens Polish culture.[9]

The takeover. Presidential and parliamentary elections were scheduled for September–October 2005. Six months in advance of the polls, Father Rydzyk, the founder and director of the fundamentalist Radio Maryja, put together a political party called the Patriotic Movement, building it on the foundation of the pre-existing Circles of Radio Maryja's Friends, consisting of some 200,000 members.[10] This initiative provoked a response from the Polish Episcopal Conference, which took up the question of behavioral rules for clergymen, but declined to discipline the wayward Rydzyk at that time.[11]

The Patriotic Movement was not, in fact, in the running; nor was the post-communist SLD, which shriveled to near nullibicity. But as late as September 10, 2005, the weekly magazine *Polityka* reported that Donald Tusk, candidate of the fiscally conservative Civic Platform (PO), enjoyed a 23% lead over his nearest rival, Lech Kaczyński, mayor of Warsaw and candidate of the intolerant Law and Justice Party (PiS).[12] More conservative bishops, however, unblushingly backed Kaczyński, with Bishop Józef Zawitowski exhorting Poles over state radio and television, "Let us make a wise choice. Let law mean law and justice mean justice."[13] The indefatigable Rydzyk also let his radio audience know his preferences, urging listeners, "We must vote for those who are in favor of supporting life, those who respect the Ten Commandments, those who back families made up of a woman and a man."[14]

Tusk, who had expressed some sympathy for gays and lesbians, went down to defeat in the runoff on October 23, 2005, garnering only 46.8% of the vote against PiS candidate Lech Kaczyński's 52.8%. Perhaps inspired by the American Republicans' "slash and spend" approach to fiscal responsibility, Kaczyński announced that he favored cutting taxes and boosting family benefits and retirement contributions.[15] The Law and Justice Party also emerged first in the parliamentary poll. Savoring his victory, Kaczyński promised to see to it that the state would be "rebuilt and cleansed,"[16] called for "a consensus based on truth,"[17] and revealed that he intended to bring about "a great change in our political life and society."[18] Judging from an opinion poll conducted by the CBOS polling agency, many Poles may be ready for the kind of "purification" that the president-elect seemed to have in mind. Reportedly, as of December 2005, more than half of all Poles believe that an authoritarian government can sometimes be better than a democratic one, while 31% of Poles associate democracy with chaos.[19]

Kaczyński took office as president on October 31, 2005, naming, as prime minister, 36-year-old Kazimierz Marcinkiewicz, a former cabinet chief for Prime Minister Jerzy Buzek. One of his first acts as prime minister, taken four days later, was to declare the abolition of the office for gender equality. He met on the same day with Bishop Piotr Libera, Secretary-General of the Polish Episcopal Council, in order to outline to the cleric his government's plans .[20] The women's rights group OSKA read this as a sign of troubles to come. Two months later, in an unprecedented move, Marcinkiewicz went on the air with Radio Maryja, thereby granting an aura of approval and legitimacy to the controversial station.[21] But with the Polish primate, Cardinal Glemp, fretting that Radio Maryja was splitting the church and the Vatican rebuking Rydzyk for dabbling in politics without written church authorization,[22] Marcinkiewicz's broadcast over Radio Maryja (rather than over Radio Puls or Radio Józef, both closer to the Polish ecclesiastical mainstream) signaled not so much an alliance of throne and altar as an alliance between the right-wing political establishment and the extreme-right wing of the Catholic community in Poland. This conclusion was confirmed and underlined when, in early February 2006, thanks to the mediation of Radio Maryja, the Law and Justice Party concluded a coalition agreement with the homophobic League of Polish Families (led by Roman Giertych) and the populist Self-Defense Party (led by Andrzej Lepper).[23]

Life unworthy of life? There are an estimated two million gays and lesbians in Poland, making up about 5% of the population.[24] In spite of this, a large majority of Poles consider homosexuality "abnormal," even "degenerate," something which should not be accepted by society. About one in every two Poles would like legislation to ban homosexuality—in spite of the fact that the EU requires both the decriminalization of homosexuality and legal guarantees against discrimination.[25] But gays, lesbians, and various sympathizers have been fighting an uphill battle for several years to gain some measure of equality (which is to say, less inequality) for persons in same-sex relationships. In April 2004, some 1,200 gay activists staged a march in the city of Kraków, only to have it degenerate into violence between marchers on the one side, and local rednecks and police on the other. In May 2004 there was a march by gay activists again in Kraków, which ended in chaos. Six months later, a peaceful march by several hundred gays in Poznań, in western Poland, came to an abrupt end when local football fans began to pelt the marchers with stones.[26] Then, in March 2005, between 500 and 1,000 women marched in the freezing cold down Warsaw's streets to demand a liberalization of abortion laws. They also linked discrimination against gays and lesbians with discrimination against women and demanded an end to sexism.[27]

In the meantime, Senator Maria Szyszkowska (SLD), a professor of philosophy at the University of Warsaw, had begun in secret to prepare a draft "Law on Registered Partnerships." By July 2003, she was ready to propose it to her colleagues. In the version presented to a subcommittee of the Senate, the bill guaranteed same-sex couples all the rights enjoyed by heterosexual couples (such as the right to be consulted about surgical procedures being considered for an unconscious loved one) except the right to adopt children. The senator told me, in July 2004, that she omitted this only because she felt that, given attitudes in Poland, a bill which would have assured gay couples of the right of adoption would have no chance at all of passage.[28] The Senate, in fact, approved the bill on December 3, 2004 by a vote of 38 to 23, with 15 abstentions, and forwarded it to the Sejm for review.[29] The Polish Ecumenical Council, which includes both the Catholic Church and other Christian churches, issued a letter in March 2005, when the bill was still under discussion, in which it charged that the bill, if adopted by the Sejm, would "call into question the very foundation of social life,"[30] although the Council failed to explain what evidence there was for this conclusion. Opposed by the church, the bill failed to win sufficient support in the Sejm, and died there. But, in recognition of her courageous efforts on behalf of gays and lesbians, in the course of which she had to endure death threats and the cancellation of a radio program she had had for years, Senator Szyszkowska was nominated for the Nobel Peace Prize in May 2005.[31]

Meanwhile, Lech Kaczyński, then mayor of Warsaw, banned an 'Equality Parade' which the Campaign Against Homophobia wanted to stage in Poland's capital in June 2005, but gave permission to the intolerant League of Polish Families to stage a so-called 'Normality Parade,' the sole purpose of which was to oppose equality for gays and lesbians.[32] Wojciech Wierzejski, a prominent figure in the League, urged the 800 participants in the anti-gay parade to refuse to employ homosexuals—in other words, to violate EU standards on discrimination. Significantly, the proportion of Poles in favor of EU membership had been in decline for a number of years.[33]

Senator Szyszkowska took part in the above-mentioned march in Kraków in May 2004, and Deputy Prime Minister Izabela Jaruga-Nowacka joined some 2,500 other people in the march in Warsaw in June 2005, in defiance of the mayoral ban. But on both occasions, as well as on the occasion of a November 2005 march in Poznań, there was violence, attributed to the instigation of the League of Polish Families and unnamed religious youth organizations,[34] and some of those opposed to the marchers in Kraków hurled acid at them. At the Poznań march, police arrested dozens of marchers, but there was no mention whether police had arrested any of those who had pelted the marchers with eggs.[35] The Catholic hierarchy was quick to condemn the gay activists, but, to the best of my knowledge, have not raised their voices in protest against the assaults on gays committed in the name of Catholic values and allegedly in defense of the family.[36] As for the anti-gay protestors, they shouted slogans such as "Euthanasia for Gays, Concentration Camps for Lesbians,"[37] thus demonstrating that they had not advanced beyond the notions held by the Nazis in the Third Reich, where local eugenic "wisdom" held that there was some life which was not "worthy" of life. Indeed, the online posting of names and e-mail addresses of 24 alleged gays and lesbians on the webpage of the aforementioned Wierzejewski, a deputy in the European Parliament, was judged to constitute a threat and was taken up by the Public Prosecutor's Office in August 2005.[38]

By this point, the European Parliament was taking note of developments in Poland, where homophobia was increasingly welcome in public and where violence against gays and lesbians was not criticized either by the parties in power or by Catholic bishops. Indeed, reports of violence against gays in Poland increased in the months following Kaczyński's inauguration as president.[39] In January 2006, having in mind problems of this nature in

Poland and Latvia as well as the Czech Republic (in spite of some important differences in the Czech case), the European Parliament issued a resolution calling on member countries to oppose "homophobic hate speech or incitement to hatred and violence" and to treat gays and lesbians with "respect, dignity, and protection."[40] Poland's bishops rejected the resolution, however, arguing that the resolution "infringes [on] basic laws of nature and imperils marriage and the family."[41] For his part, Archbishop Józef Życiński of Lublin added that he and other bishops deplored the fact that the European Parliament was allegedly "trying to intervene in the condition of Polish souls."[42] For the Polish bishops, thus, divine law is higher than international law, and Poland should, accordingly, ignore the international accords which it signs when they are considered (by the bishops) to contradict the will of God. The fact that this view is now mainstream in Poland suggests that Poland has become, at this point, a full-fledged clerical democracy, in which people may indeed vote, but not about those matters which are rooted in longstanding religious traditions, even if they are traditions of intolerance and bigotry.

A polarized society. About 95% of Poles declare themselves as Catholics[43] and 83% of Poles consider their religion to be a critical element in their personal identities.[44] Yet, in spite of this, opinions in Poland are sharply divided over values associated with the Catholic Church. Some 50% of Poles, for instance, would like to see the church permit divorce, while 42% are opposed to any liberalization in this sphere. 24% of Poles support the idea of women priests, with 66% opposed. Fully 92% of the population would like to see sex education introduced in the state schools (a measure which the church opposes).[45] Again, while 35% feel that the law on abortion should be relaxed, fully 53% are against any easing of restrictions here. And finally, just 22% of Poles want to see liberalization in the area of same-sex unions, with 67% supporting the church's view in this sphere.[46] As one would expect, persons with higher education predominate among the liberals, while those with only primary school education tend to be more conservative on these issues.

In a post-electoral post mortem, Michał Syska, deputy chair of the Polish Social Democrats (SdPL), looked to the future in search of a viable alternative vision to what he called Kaczyński's "conservative-national model." In his view, the Civic Platform, written off as a "liberal" party by Rydzyk, was too conservative in some ways and, in any event, virtually indistinguishable from the PiS on issues such as lustration, decommunization, and, appearances notwithstanding, taxation policies. For Syska, the point of departure is to identify the problem: "the violation of civic rights and restriction of democracy" being perpetrated by the right-wing coalition and its allies.[47] From there, it is necessary, Syska added, to distinguish between "imagined threats" (such as gays and lesbians) and the real threats to Polish society, among whom he counted the newly elected president and his PiS.

Meanwhile, Poland came under sharp criticism from the European Parliament in June 2006, when the parliament issued a resolution highlighting problems of racist, xenophobic, anti-Semitic, and homophobic intolerance in Poland and three other European countries.[48] In response, Marek Jurek, speaker of the Sejm, rejected the resolution for being "supportive of homosexual ideology"[49]—as if sexual preference were a matter of ideology rather than nature. Then, in early July, Maciej Giertych, a Polish member of the European parliament, apparently responding to that body's resolution, rose to sing the praises of deceased Spanish fascist dictator, General Francisco Franco. Father of the more famous minister of education, Maciej Giertych told his fellow MEPs, "The presence of such people in European politics as Franco guaranteed the maintenance of traditional values in Europe and we lack such statesmen today. Christian Europe is losing against atheistic socialists today and this has to change."[50] Tolerance, queen of the liberal virtues, is apparently, for Giertych, an atheistic principle having nothing to do with Christianity.

LIBERAL DEMOCRACY/THE LAIC STATE—
THE CASE OF THE CZECH REPUBLIC

In the Czech Republic, the concept of the "laic state" is dominant, even though, as in any society, there are diverse currents, including, in the Czech Republic, currents critical of the laic model. Illustrative of the difference is the fact that, in the Czech Republic (by comparison with Slovakia), the Catholic Church has been unable to obtain the introduction of religious instruction per se into the public school system. Instead, a class on civic education was introduced. The course was designed to inform schoolchildren about morals and ethics, and to provide some basic information about religious life in the country. Indeed, local critics such as A. Ambruz have insisted that the state (and hence the state school system) should play no role in moral education and that the religious organizations should accomplish this task outside publicly financed institutions.[51]

Property restitution. One of the challenges faced by the Czech government, at least where religious communities are concerned, has been the question of the restitution of property confiscated by the communists. In the first three years after the collapse of the communist system in Czechoslovakia, the government returned about 250 buildings and land plots in Bohemia and Moravia to Catholic religious orders and congregations, but the church claimed title to an additional 3,300 buildings and 600,000 acres of wooded and unwooded land.[52] The church has had its advocates in the parliament, but some parties have categorically opposed any restitution of church property.[53] The first attempt to restore property to the church, attempted in April 1992 before the parliamentary elections which sounded the death knell for a united Czechoslovakia, failed in the federal parliament by just three votes. Interestingly enough, those three votes were cast by deputies from Slovakia where, by the mid-1990s, the issue of property restitution would be resolved.[54]

After the Czechoslovak state split in two, a commission was appointed in Prague to draw up an inventory of church property as of 1994 and make recommendations for the return of property to religious orders. By 2000, about 200 monasteries and convents previously confiscated by the communists had been returned to their original owners.[55] Where diocesan property was concerned, however, progress on legislation slowed to a standstill, and tensions grew between the Catholic hierarchy and Czech Prime Minister Václav Klaus.[56] By way of a compromise, Cardinal Vlk suggested the hierarchy would be content with the return of just 800 of the 3,300 buildings in dispute.[57] But the government was disinclined to move quickly, and, for that matter, about 50% of Czechs were said to be opposed to the restitution of property to the church (according to opinion polls conducted in the early 1990s).[58] Moreover, even though, in 1998, Miloš Zeman, chair of the Social Democratic Party and the incoming prime minister, declared that the government would increase the salaries being paid to priests and ministers by 15%, priests' salaries would still remain well below the national average.[59] This largesse would be purchased at a price, since Zeman also announced that his government would cease all talk of property restitution to religious communities, except for the Jewish community. When Miloslav Cardinal Vlk, archbishop of Prague, insisted that talks nonetheless continue, Deputy Prime Minister Pavel Rychetský accused the archbishop of "disloyalty" and "communist"-style behavior.[60] For their part, the Christian Democrats characterized Minister of Culture Pavel Dostál (Social Demo-

crat) as a "bolshevik" after he challenged the legitimacy of even those resti-
tutions already authorized. Meanwhile, Vlk and Dostál continued to exchange caustic comments; church-state relations seemed to remain at a low
point.[61] Dostál passed away in 2005, being succeeded in office by Jana
Řepová. However, Martin Horálek, a spokesperson for the Catholic Episcopal Conference, said he did not believe the change at the Ministry of
Culture would make much difference for the church.[62]

By that point, the continued deterioration of church facilities was ex-
erting a pressure on Catholic authorities and suggesting a new approach. In
the Karlovy Vary region, for example, almost half of the 134 churches owned
by the Roman Catholic Church were described as "very dilapidated" and in
serious need of repair as of October 2005; 8% were thought to be near collapse.[63] Hence, although at one time the church may have dreamed of re-
gaining not only the bulk of the property confiscated by the communists but
even some of the property confiscated by Emperor Josef II in the late 18th
century,[64] by early 2005, Czech Catholic bishops were offering to give up
their claims to property restitution in exchange for a commitment from the
state to pay the church 1 billion *korune* ($43.5 million) annually for the next
half-century.[65]

A state treaty. After the fall of communism in East Central Europe,
the Holy See set a priority on signing concordats—state treaties with governments in the region—in order to afford the church certain legal guarantees. Work on a draft treaty between the Czech Republic and the Vatican
began in 2000, and two years later, the text was finalized and subsequently
forwarded to the Czech parliament. The Chamber of Deputies rejected it
by a vote of 177 to 110, on the argument that the treaty was disadvantageous
to the Czech state and violated the equality of faiths guaranteed under the
constitution.[66] The treaty had proposed to regulate the church's activities in
education, health and social care, prison services, and the military.[67] As of
February 2006, the treaty was on hold, with passage considered unlikely before the June 2006 general elections.[68]

Controversies over legislation. In 2001, the Czech parliament
passed a new law governing religious communities, which came into effect
on January 1, 2002. This law gave the Ministry of Culture the authority to
register religious charities and enterprises but church hierarchs objected
that the law imposed inappropriate restrictions on the church's operation of
its sundry social projects. The church's claim seemed to be confirmed when,
in October 2003, the Constitutional Court ruled that the ministry had acted

improperly in declining to register an enterprise operated by the Catholic Church in the town of Lipnik nad Bečvou.[69]

During 2005, controversy flared between the Catholic Church and the government over three proposed measures: a bill requiring religious organizations to register their charities, schools, and hospitals with the state and tightening government control over these sectors ("the amendment")[70]; a bill permitting scientists to work with "embryonic stem cells from surplus or damaged embryos"[71]; and a bill on the registration of same-sex partnerships. The Catholic Church opposed all three measures, arguing that "the amendment" violated democratic principles[72] and that the bill regulating stem cell research was morally unacceptable because "no human being, including embryos, can become [the] means to achieve benefits for other people."[73] In spite of the bishops' opposition, the amendment was passed by the parliament in June 2005 and signed into law by President Klaus in December 2005, and the Chamber of Deputies approved the bill on stem cell research in February 2006, forwarding it to the Senate for review.[74]

As for the bill concerning same-sex partnerships, the measure had come before the Chamber of Deputies already in February 2005, at which time it was defeated by one vote. The Gay and Lesbian League of the Czech Republic therefore mounted a fresh petition drive and, by September 2005, the new bill had been endorsed by the petition committee of the Chamber of Deputies. As the Chamber itself began to discuss the measure, opponents claimed that granting gays and lesbians equal rights (or rather, less unequal rights) with heterosexuals would weaken the traditional family. Unswayed by this vague claim, the Chamber of Deputies voted in December 2005 to legalize the registration of same-sex partnerships. Under the bill, a partner would have the right to be informed about his or her partner's condition of health, to be consulted about medical procedures on an unconscious partner, and to inherit the property of a deceased partner.[75]

Archbishop Jan Graubner characterized the prospect that gay and lesbian couples might enjoy these rights "a disaster, another blow to the family which has already been in crisis."[76] Bishop Vojtěch Cikrle (of Brno) was more revealing in warning that the bill "could contribute to chaos in value orientation"[77]—code for doubts about Catholic teachings concerning sexual morality. Catholic opposition notwithstanding, the Senate passed the bill on same-sex partnerships in January 2006.[78] President Klaus vetoed the measure in mid-February, however, leaving its ultimate fate uncertain. Although the Chamber of Deputies could override the presidential veto, it would need 101 votes to do so, or 15 more than the 86 it had mustered to pass it in the first place.[79] With some 62% of Czechs in favor of registered partnerships for same-sex couples,[80] Prime Minister Jiří Paroubek (Social Democrat) felt confident that the parliament would override the presidential veto. In fact, the Chamber of Deputies did so on March 15, 2006 by a narrow vote, mustering the 101 votes needed and provoking a hostile response from church circles.[81]

A HYBRID: VALUES IN CONTENTION—SLOVAKIA

By contrast with Poland and the Czech Republic, post-communist Slovakia is neither a clerical democracy nor a laic state. It is, rather, a democracy in which the clerical and laic models compete, in which each side is able to win occasional victories, with neither achieving hegemony. The result is a kind of hybrid; neither side is satisfied. The Catholic Church has had its victories, such as the restitution act of October 27, 1993, which returned some properties to the church. These properties included forests, meadows, and some church buildings, but excluded properties on which state hospitals, social service providers, and schools had been constructed, as well as properties operated by cooperative farms and trading companies.[82] After the law was passed, Ján Cardinal Korec, the bishop of Nitra, thanked the parliament for having "shown a sense of justice" and for having "achieved a leading [moral] position in Central and Eastern Europe."[83]

Controveries over police harassment and religious instruction. Given their focus on getting their former property back and on obtaining other concessions from the government, the bishops were slow to react to the growing authoritarianism of Prime Minister Vladimír Mečiar, who served in office intermittently between 1992 and 1998. But there was at least one priest, Father Ján Suchán, who spoke out. Beginning in February 1993, Radio Twist, a private radio station, began broadcasting Suchán's weekly sermons. Suchán's homilies were critical not only of the Mečiar government but also of the Catholic hierarchy which, at that time, hesitated to condemn Mečiar openly.[84] After Mečiar returned to office toward the end of 1994, he undertook efforts, among other things, to purge the civil service and the media of his critics, to cut the salaries of judges not considered "reliable," to restrict freedom of speech, and even to expel opposition deputies from the parliament on the pretext of alleged electoral fraud. The bishops felt that they could no longer remain silent and, from 1995 to 1998, Bishop Rudolf Baláž of Banská Bystrica, the chairman of the Slovak Episcopal Conference, took public stands against the government's racism, against the infamous "Protection of the Republic" law approved in early 1996 (providing for the criminal prosecution of anyone convicted of spreading misinformation about the Slovak state), and against other authoritarian policies.[85] During these years, the church found itself reenacting patterns of behavior it had been forced to learn in the communist era. As the church spoke out, it found itself targeted for harassment by the government. As early as 1995, for example, the Slovak secret service (SIS) reportedly sent an agent, under a pseudonym, to purchase an antique triptych belonging to Bishop Baláž's office; the ensuing sale was entirely legal, but the SIS now charged that the church had illegally sold a national treasure.[86] The gambit was designed to discredit the hierarchy, but the church reacted defiantly. On August 18, church officials accused the government of communist-style practices, and three days later some 3,000 Catholics took to the streets of Banská Bystrica in protest.[87] In mid-1997, preparations for a basic treaty between the Slovak Republic and the Vatican got underway. But progress on the treaty was allegedly obstructed by the Mečiar cabinet's insistence that the government be notified in advance of any bishops being appointed by the Vatican.[88] Thus, it was only after Mečiar's third fall from office that the draft treaty was finalized and signed.

In 1998, as a result of parliamentary elections, a government headed by Mikuláš Dzurinda came to power. Even before the end of the year, the newly elected parliament voted "to establish equal financial conditions for state and church schools, to found a Catholic university, and to conclude an agreement with the Vatican."[89] Of course, as already noted, a draft treaty had been ready for signing already in 1997 and was, in due course, signed. In subsequent years, the church engaged in a series of turf battles, succeeding in obtaining the removal of yoga classes from the school curriculum, in blocking a liberalization of rules on abortion (which would have allowed the abortion of fetuses found to have serious genetic defects), and in scotching efforts to legalize same-sex unions.[90]

Parliamentary deputies of the Slovak Communist Party recoiled at what they considered a clericalization of Slovak public life and objected to the diversion of tax revenues to religious organizations. Accordingly, in spring 2003, communist deputies demanded an end to the state's financial support for religious communities and an unambiguous affirmation of the separation of church and state.[91] Meanwhile, the treaty with the Vatican finally came up for a vote in the parliament. Under the treaty, state schools are obliged to make religious instruction available, although children may sign up for a class in ethics instead. There were two aspects to the bill which were considered controversial: the fact that religious instruction was to be offered in state schools at all, with state financing on top of it, and the appeals registered immediately by ten non-Catholic religious bodies for equal access.[92] The liberal New Citizens Alliance (ANO) opposed the bill, however, as did the Smer Party and the Communist Party of Slovakia, and it was only in January 2004 that it was finally passed into law. When the battle was already lost, Róbert Fico, chairman of Smer, expressed his consternation that the civic principle was thereby being violated.[93] Up to this point, thus, the Catholic Church seemed to be having its way in the country and Slovakia seemed to be adhering to some variant of the clerical model.

Spiritual corruption and the threat of abortion. From the standpoint of the Catholic Church, same-sex partnerships and abortions are sinful manifestations of a decadent age, and the legalization of these "sins" is the mark of the spiritual corruption of the laic or secular state. Insofar as the European Union has favored liberalization in these spheres, the Slovak Catholic bishops have expressed their concern that EU membership "must not threaten the preservation of traditional Christian values in the country."[94] But, from the standpoint of the church, there are threats all around. So-called "reality shows" on television are, according to Slovakia's bishops, not just bad taste or bad art, but in fact "spread moral and cultural decline."[95] Sex education in the schools is not a contribution to a successful marriage, according to the bishops, but "reduces partnership to the level of sex only, while ignoring the context of married life, parenthood and responsibility."[96] Same-sex partnerships likewise fall under the rubric of threats to traditional values. And, on this subject, Slovaks were less inclined than Czechs to favor same-sex partnerships, but more inclined than Poles to do so.[97]

Controversy over abortion proved to be an explosive issue and, in early 2006, actually brought down the Slovak government when the church's advocates failed to win that particular battle. The controversy over abortion can be traced back to February 2001, when the Christian Democratic Party (KDH) sought to incorporate a ban on abortion in the constitution; the measure was defeated in the parliament that same month by a vote of 59 to 44, with 37 abstentions.[98] The tide subsequently turned, as the ANO pushed through an amendment to the abortion law, liberalizing it further; where the law had formerly allowed abortion only until the 12th week of pregnancy, the amended law allowed abortion up to the 24th week, in the event of "health risk reasons" such as a genetic damage.[99]

Arguing that "instinctive opposition to the termination of an innocent human life, whether we call it an embryo, [a] foetus, or [an] unborn child, should be reflected in legislation,"[100] the KDH developed a two-pronged strategy to fight the new law. On the one hand, the party brought the measure before the Constitutional Court, arguing that the law was contrary to the constitution. On the other hand, it worked with the Vatican to prepare a treaty to guarantee every citizen (e.g., physicians) the right to refuse to provide services (e.g., abortions) for reasons of conscience. The Constitutional Court met on September 4, 2003 to review the case but adjourned before it could take any action. Sixteenth months later, Chief Justice Ján Mazák declared the indefinite postponement of any resolution of the case on the argument that the court had two vacancies and could not make a determination in the absence of a full court.[101]

Then, in late 2005, the proposed treaty on exercising conscientious objection to abortion came before an EU review board, in the light of Slovakia's accession to that body. The review board concluded that the treaty violated the principles of democracy and human rights because such a right, anchored in a treaty, could result in women being unable to obtain abortions even if such abortions would be permitted under Slovak law.[102] In the wake of this report, Foreign Minister Eduard Kukan refused to sign the treaty, which meant that it was not forwarded to the parliament for review. Barely a week later, KDH leaders announced that they were quitting the governing coalition, which in turn resulted in the fall of the government of Mikuláš Dzurinda.[103] Where the KDH has championed a clerical democracy, in which Catholic values would be protected by law, the left-oriented parties in Slovakia have championed a laic state. Not surprisingly, Slovak bishops advised their faithful, in a pastoral letter read at masses on May 28, 2006, to vote for parties that respect Christian values and to reject parties supportive of same-sex partnerships or legal access to abortion.[104]

The church in Slovak society. Practicing Catholics are significantly less numerous than nominal Catholics in Slovakia. In the 2001 census, for instance, 84% of Slovaks said that they were religious believers, and 69% of the total declared that they were Catholics. But only 20% of the population are practicing Catholics.[105] Moreover, while the Catholic Church is certainly respected in Slovak society, a 2003 opinion poll found that it ranked as only the third most trusted institution among Slovaks (with 48.3% trusting the church), behind the army (66.5%) and the National Bank (54%), though well ahead of the parliament (32.8%) and the government (20.4%).[106]

At the same time, the church has engaged itself on the side of the poor, noting that Slovakia has (as of November 2005) the highest poverty rate among EU members and urging legislators to adopt measures to narrow the gap between the rich and the poor.[107] Poverty, in turn, contributes to unstable family life, according to the bishops, thereby threatening the "traditional model of a satisfied and stable family."[108]

CONCLUSION

In the foregoing chapter, I have outlined three models of church-state condominium: clericalism (church dominant), the laic state (state dominant), and hybrid (in which neither state nor church is clearly dominant and in which rival points of view concerning the optimal model for condominium are advanced). I have also suggested that only the laic state is fully compatible with the principles of tolerance, equality, and neutrality of the state in matters of religion—central elements in the liberal project—and that, in the Polish case at least, the Catholic Church has, in fact, waged war against all six liberal principles. Clericalism is not necessarily anti-democratic; rather, it offers its own model of democracy: clerical democracy. This is a democracy in which Divine Law, as interpreted by the dominant religious body, is beyond question. It is also a system in which persons outside the graces of the dominant religious body may be excluded from enjoying fully equal rights.

When, as in the United States, anti-abortion activists arrogate to themselves the right, indeed the duty, to murder physicians who perform abortions—together with their patients—or to take part in actions to block patients from reaching a given medical facility, those activists are appealing beyond positive law to the purported will of God; they are usually also acting against the precepts of their own nominal religious association. Similarly, when American anti-gay activist Pete Peters called upon Christians "to campaign state by state (as the homosexuals have done) for a law that would make the death penalty mandatory for gays and lesbians,"[109] he is evoking the authority of a wrathful God to whom obedience to ancient traditions is more valuable than human life itself. Peters is a quintessential example of judgmental religious fundamentalism.

Clericalism, whether in its conservative Catholic form, its Christian Right incarnation, as manifested in Islamic fundamentalism, or orthodox Jewish fundamentalism, is only one of the ideas competing in the religio-political marketplace. To begin with, there are liberal (or reformed) currents within all of these religious traditions—currents pleading for tolerance and coexistence. These currents are potentially fully compatible with the liberal project, since liberalism is not anti-religious; it is merely anti-clerical. To be more explicit, what liberalism opposes is the notion that one religious faith may dictate its moral and social agenda to the entire society, including persons who are not members of that faith. But liberalism, as I stressed already in chapter 2, is evolving, and being extended in new directions. Some dimensions of this extension of the liberal project are explored in chapter 7.

7

THE FATE OF WOMEN IN
POST-1989 EASTERN EUROPE

The argument presented here consists of three parts: first, that the situation of women in Eastern Europe has deteriorated on a number of significant measures since the collapse of communism in 1989; second, that the deterioration in women's equality and rights is related to a broader context in which conservative forces promote so-called traditional values, including homophobia and sexual intolerance in general; and third, that the direction the struggle for gender equality must take is beyond liberalism and beyond democracy—recognizing that, though these two Enlightenment legacies have been enormously positive in the past, liberalism has increasingly been interpreted too narrowly and only a broader interpretation can lead forward; indeed, democracy has come face to face with serious problems with which it has been unable to cope, except in a dysfunctional way. This is not a call for authoritarian solutions but rather a suggestion that what passes for democracy is, from an Aristotelian perspective, as well as from a feminist perspective, a travesty of democratic principles.

DETERIORATION OF THE
STATUS OF WOMEN

The conditions under which the transition from communism was undertaken were less than ideal, and the result has been "disruption and hardship for large groups of people."[1] Layoffs from work, economic disorganization and decline, the spread of organized crime, widespread poverty, a proliferation of corruption, and the sale of capital stock at below-market prices to foreign concerns—these have been among the most salient problems in the economic sector. Ten years after the collapse of communism, at least 20% of the population of Eastern Europe lived below the poverty line, with the highest rates of poverty to be found in the Serbian Republic, the Republic of Serbia (including Kosova), Albania, and Moldova, where an estimated 55% live below the poverty line.[2] Even in Hungary and Poland, which have been doing relatively better among East European countries in transition, there are pockets of poverty.

Women have suffered more than men in all countries in transition. According to UNECE, female employment shrank at faster rates than male employment during the years 1985–97 in all countries for which adequate data are available (Poland, Czech Republic, Hungary, Slovenia, Estonia, Latvia, Lithuania, and Russia); in Hungary, for example, female employment dropped by 40% in these years while male employment declined by 30%.[3] The collapse of the existing pension systems—most dramatically in Serbia, Bosnia-Herzegovina, and Albania—affected both women and men, though the fact that women are generally forced to retire, on the average, five years earlier than men in the region has made pension reform a more troubling problem for women.

There are confirmed reports of a tangible increase in domestic violence throughout this region in the years after 1989, which one observer attributes to "increased alcohol consumption on the part of men due to feelings of inadequacy—both as providers and as men."[4] But this approach provides, at best, an incomplete explanation of the rise in domestic violence since the collapse of communism. A more complete explanation would also mention

- *the delegitimation of communist ideology and, with it, the communist claim that gender equality should enjoy a priority.*
- *the increased activity on the part of traditional ecclesiastical institutions such as the Roman Catholic Church in Poland, Croatia, Slovenia, and Slovakia and the Orthodox Church in Russia, Romania, and Serbia, to the extent that they promote a "traditional" role for women in which women are urged to see themselves essentially as servants to their husbands and children.*
- *the influx of neo-Protestant and New Age religions, many of them subscribing to extremely inegalitarian models of gender relations.*

- *the proliferation of pornography in the region, encouraging some women and some men to view sex and sexuality as a commodity, thereby contributing to the dehumanization of women.*
- *the dynamic of nationalism, which has affected the post-Yugoslav region above all.*

Where the role of nationalism is concerned, George Mosse's research has identified the organic nexus between nationalism and antifeminism,[5] while Žarana Papić has pointed to a "structural connection between ethnic and gender violence" through which women "are colonized and instrumentalized in their 'natural' function as 'birth-machines'" and in which women of the "enemy nation [are] . . . reified into the targets of [intended] destruction."[6] The association of nationalism with traditional models of gender relations is also illustrated by the activities of Don Anto Baković, a semi-retired Croatian priest whose Croatian Population Movement committed itself to the goal of "sav[ing] the Croatian nation from extinction"[7] and undertook to mount a propaganda campaign against what it called "the anti-life mentality."[8] Abortion became a favorite target for nationalists, for example in Hungary, where a group called Pacem in Utero (Peace in the Uterus) described abortion as a betrayal of the nation and called feminists "mother killers."[9]

The economic context. The deterioration of conditions for women may be situated in a broader economic and social context. In Serbia, for example, economic conditions have contributed to a dramatic rise in suicides and attempted suicides. Andjelka Milić, a professor of sociology at the University of Belgrade, conducted a poll among Serbs in spring 2002 and reported that "two thirds of families polled said that they feel like losers in all aspects of life," with many declaring that they have "nothing to live for."[10] In Bosnia, unemployment is estimated at about 40%, with high levels of mental disorder, anxiety, and aggression. The number of suicides has also been rising here, with more than twice as many suicides in the Serbian sector (in 2000) as in the Bosniak-Croat sector.[11]

In Bulgaria, in spite of buoyant promises by the government, income was reported to be lower in 2002 than it had been in 1986–90.[12] Indeed, a report published in 2002 fretted that "the country is in danger of going the way of Argentina, as a large proportion of the population sinks into poverty."[13] Symptomatic of the country's economic uncertainty was that about 40% of its gross domestic product was thought to be in the so-called gray economy, which is to say, beyond easy government control.[14] In neighboring Romania, per capita income was likewise lower in 2001 than it had been in 1986–90. Moreover, some 45% of Romanians still lived below the poverty line in 2001.[15] As one observer put it, "Most Romanians still barely get by in grinding poverty and believe the only way out is by being corrupt."[16] Among the social problems plaguing Romania is human trafficking, with large numbers of non-Europeans, especially Iraqis and Afghans, being spirited into Romania without legal papers or any provision for employment.[17] Per capita income has also declined in recent years in Macedonia (where it was lower in 2002 than in 1986–90) and in Albania (where it was likewise lower in 2002 than in 1981–85).[18] As of November 2000, about 20% of Macedonia's population lived below the official poverty line,[19] but the figure today might well be higher because of the impact of the fighting during 2001 and other problems.

Unemployment and economic inequality. As of 1996/97, women were about 20% more likely than men to be unemployed in several countries of the region, while women's wages were no more than 80% of men's wages in the Czech Republic, Slovakia, Poland, and Hungary and just barely more than that in Slovenia.[20] Since 1989, the cost of education has risen across Eastern Europe, health services have deteriorated, and state expenditures on child-care facilities have been radically slashed. More teenage girls are giving birth now, drug abuse and alcohol abuse are increasing, domestic violence and rape are reportedly also rising, and life expectancy for women has declined in sixteen of the countries in transition. Even where so basic a need as health insurance is concerned, there were more women in the transition societies lacking health insurance in 1998 than in 1993.[21] Female unemployment, which remains higher than male unemployment, is the result of several factors, including the closure of many child-care facilities and the discriminatory treatment meted out to women (last hired, first fired). Female migrants tend to find employment in "a limited number of typically female jobs: domestic service, casual employment, industries requiring abundant labour, the leisure industry, the sex industry and more especially prostitution."[22]

Where economic success stories are concerned, there are fewer women entrepreneurs than men entrepreneurs in all transition countries. In the Czech Republic, for example, only 9% of employed women are entrepreneurs, as compared with 18.8% of men; in Hungary, the figures are 9.6% for women and 18.7% for men, and in Romania 17.4% for women and 32.6% for men. In Slovenia, which is considered more progressive in some dimensions, the differential between the rate of female entrepreneurship (6.5%)

and male entrepreneurship (15.3%) is actually the greatest.[23] In Poland, some employers have demanded that prospective female employees provide medical certification that they are not pregnant and sign a contract pledging not to become pregnant for at least two years.[24]

In August 1999, survey research was conducted among 210 Polish women in the former voivodships of Szczecin, Katowice, and Białystok at the request of the Federation for Women and Family Planning. More than 60% of these women reported that their overall situation had either deteriorated or stagnated since 1989. Some 40% of respondents said that their living conditions had deteriorated, 40% that the quality of health care service had declined, 44% that the financial situation in their families had deteriorated, 50% that they had fewer professional opportunities than a decade earlier, and 70% that prices had increased in real terms.[25] On the other hand, respondents also noted improvements in some areas. Some 34.8% said that legal protection in general had improved, 45.2% that possibilities for children's education had improved, 51% that there was more personal freedom, 52% that women had more rights to express their opinions, and 87% that there were better supplies of commodities in shops. Putting these two sets together, one may conclude that Polish women saw a general deterioration in economic conditions but a general improvement in political freedom. It should also be noted that negative assessments were more often given by those who were older or who had more than two children, while optimistic assessments were more often given by more affluent women, especially those having no children.

Political participation. In communist times, women constituted 20% of all mayors and 45% of all judges in the German Democratic Republic, 23% of all parliamentary deputies in Poland, 25–30% of all parliamentary deputies in Hungary, and 19.5% of deputies in the assemblies of the republics and autonomous provinces of late Tito-era Yugoslavia.[26] The contrast with comparable figures in the early postcommunist era is striking. As of 1999, the average proportion of women in parliaments in the transition countries was less than 10%.[27] In Slovenia (as of 1996), only 8% of the deputies in the parliament were women, while in Serbia (as of 1990–93), only 1.6% of parliamentary deputies were women.[28] The proportion of women among candidates for national parliaments has been as low as 20% and, except for a few left-wing parties, the political parties generally abhor the use of gender quotas. As a result, female representation in national parliaments has been low. In 1994, for example, women accounted for 15.0% of the deputies in the Czech parliament, 13.0% of deputies in the Polish Sejm, 12.0%

of deputies in the Slovak parliament, 8.3% of deputies in the Hungarian parliament, and 7.8% of deputies in the Slovenian parliament.[29]

Many women's organizations function as either mobilization tools of male-dominated parties (as in the case of the women's organizations of Christian Democratic parties) or agents for the advancement of nationalist goals (as in the case of Macedonia's League of Albanian Women). Moreover, in the Czech case, some 95% of women's organizations are not concerned with politics at all,[30] while both the label "feminism" and the feminist agenda have been so thoroughly deprecated that few advocates of women's equality dare to refer to themselves as feminists.[31] It is no accident that, when a group of politically motivated women in Prague wanted to establish a center to serve as a focal point for their activities, they chose the neutral name Gender Studies Center. Slovenia provides an even more striking case, with Ljubljana's leading center for the study of gender relations, gender stereotypes, and sex discrimination calling itself the Peace Institute.

It has sometimes been argued that it does not make any difference whether a representative is male or female, and that a male representative can just as well represent women as a female deputy, though the fact that it is always women who are underrepresented in parliaments, rather than men, should give one pause. Moreover, this assumption has been challenged head-on. Magdalena Środa, a Polish feminist philosopher, has declared, for example:

> I, personally, do not wish to see a parliament, in which sit my supposed representatives (almost all) of male gender, because I am becoming convinced that we [women] really have different interests, needs, different ways of understanding the world, different hierarchies of values, aims, different conceptions of politics, the function of the family, children, different notions of upbringing, economic priorities, different role models.[32]

In fact, the representation of women in Polish parliamentary life had been declining steadily since it had reached an early high of 23% in the years 1980–85. From then, the proportion of women in the Sejm (what is today the lower house of the Polish parliament) sank to 20% in 1985–89, 13% in 1990–91, and just 10% in 1991–93, stabilizing at 13% in the years 1993–2001. But in the 1990s, women organized to change this situation. One such group, Grupa Nieformalna "Kobiety Też," emerged in 1993 and began organizing conferences and workshops, giving support to female candidates in local elections and pushing for equal treatment of women and men in media coverage. The group sought to promote both a more proportional representation of women in public life and a greater responsiveness on the part of female politicians to women's needs. When, in 2001, female representation in the Sejm rose from 13% to more than 20%, and in the Senate from 13% to 23%, Kobiety Też and other such groups saw their efforts at least temporarily crowned with success.[33]

Women's mobilization is only one factor that has arguably begun to reverse the conservative tide in at least some societies of Eastern Europe. Among the other factors, one should mention the revival of left-wing political parties in some of these countries and international pressure (all of the states in the region have either signed or succeeded to the international treaty on discrimination against women, and some have also signed an optional protocol expanding the guarantees to women). The big success stories (in relative terms, of course) in the region are Poland, where (as of 2002) women constituted more than 21% of cabinet members (the highest figure in the region), 20–23% of parliamentary deputies, and 13.2% of municipal councilors; Bulgaria, where women constituted nearly 19% of cabinet members, 26% of parliamentary deputies (the highest figure in the region), and 20% of municipal councilors (again the highest figure in the region); and Slovenia, where women constituted 20% of cabinet members, 13% of parliamentary deputies, and 12.2% of municipal councilors (see table 7.1). On the other hand, there were no women in the Czech cabinet in 2002, and women constituted less than 10% of parliamentary deputies in Albania, Macedonia, and Hungary and just 4% of municipal councilors in Croatia. Commenting on the Albanian case, Human Rights Internet noted recently that "the emergence of a more democratic society has not in fact led to greater participation of women in decision-making but to a greater exclusion of women from public life and political participation."[34]

A comparison of the East European data (table 7.1) with data from Northern and Western Europe (table 7.2) is instructive. In the Nordic countries in the same period, women comprised 28–45% of cabinet ministers and 35–43% of parliamentary deputies, while in the "Big Four" (Britain, France, Germany, and Italy) women accounted for 10–43% of cabinet ministers but only 8–31% of parliamentary deputies (Italian inclusion of women in parliamentary life being the lowest in this particular set).

Whether the Nordic countries can exert any influence in the societies of Eastern Europe is, at best, uncertain, and if there is to be any such influence, it can only be the result of special relations between the countries.

TABLE 7.1

Representation of Women in Political Bodies, Eastern Europe, 2002 (%)

	Cabinet	Parliament	Municipal Councilors	Mayors
		(uni-/bicameral)		
Albania	16.67	6	11	3
Bulgaria	18.75	26	20.0	8
Croatia	8.33	6 / 21	4.0	—
Czech Republic	0	15 / 12	—	—
Hungary	6.25	8.5	9.1*	13.0
Macedonia	5.88	6	8.4	21.4
Poland	21.43	20 / 23	13.2	5.3
Romania	20.00	7 / 12	—	3.4
Serbia	—	2.08**	—	—
Slovakia	10.00	13.3	—	16.9
Slovenia	20.00	13	12.2	4.2

— = no data
* = local representatives
** = data from spring 2000

SOURCE: *Women in Politics in the Council of Europe Member States* (Strasbourg: CoE Directorate General of Human Rights, May 2002), 59–64. The Serbian figure comes from Biljana Bijelić, "Nationalism, Motherhood, and the Reordering of Women's Power," in Sabrina P. Ramet and Vjeran Pavlaković, eds., *Serbia since 1989: Politics and Society under Milošević and After* (Seattle: University of Washington Press, 2005).

But the Nordic countries provide a model, at least, of near-equality. It is noteworthy that the Women's Rights Committee of the European Parliament has recommended that women comprise at least 40% "of all political bodies at European, national and international levels."[35] As of 2000, the European Parliament itself consisted of 30% female deputies and 70% male deputies.

   Abortion: The case of Poland. In the Czech Republic, Slovakia, Hungary, Slovenia, Croatia, Serbia and Montenegro, Bosnia-Herzegovina, Albania, Macedonia, Romania, and Bulgaria, laws on abortion are liberal, allowing women unrestricted access to abortion at least through the first twelve weeks of pregnancy. In Russia, abortion is authorized for social rea-

TABLE 7.2

Representation of Women in Political Bodies,
Nordic and West European Countries, 2002 (%)

	Cabinet	Parliament	Municipal Councilors	Mayors
		(uni-/bicameral)		
NORDIC				
Denmark	27.78*	37.99	27	—
Finland	44.44	37.50	34	—
Iceland	33.33	34.92	29**	3.0
Norway	42.11	36.97	42	—
Sweden	45.00	42.69	42	—
WESTERN EUROPE				
France	21.43	10.92	47.5	10.9
Germany	43	31.24 / 17.39	—	—
Italy	10.39	9.84 / 7.67	16.7	6.6
United Kingdom	32.58	17.91	—	—

— = no data
* = down from 45% in 2000
** = local representatives

SOURCE: *Women in Politics in the Council of Europe Member States* (Strasbourg: CoE Directorate General of Human Rights, May 2002), 26, 59–64.

sons for up to twenty-two weeks and at any point in the pregnancy for medical reasons.[36]

Abortion was legal in Poland from 1956 until 1993, when the Polish Sejm, under heavy pressure from the Catholic Church, passed a highly restrictive law. After the election of a more liberal Sejm, however, the law was liberalized in 1996, and for a few months in 1997 abortions were allowed to be conducted on social grounds (which usually meant for financial reasons). But the law was toughened once again in 1997, after a decision by the Constitutional Tribunal. The Catholic Church wanted a total ban on abortions, without exception. However, the 1997 law allows the termination of pregnancy when continuation of the pregnancy would endanger the life of the woman, when a prenatal exam reveals severe and irreversible damage to the fetus or the presence of an incurable disease, or when a state prosecutor confirms that the pregnancy is the result of a rape.[37]

The law itself is highly restrictive, but what is striking is that its application de facto has been tougher and more restrictive than the law itself, and many women who would be entitled to an abortion under the 1997 law have been denied the procedure. As a result of the restrictive legislation and the pressure from the church on the hospitals, as well as of the stigma attached by conservatives to the procedure, the number of legal abortions conducted in Poland declined from 82,137 in 1989 to just 151 in 1999. On paper, then, it appears that the church has scored a big victory in its fight against abortion. But in fact there are thought to be between 80,000 and 200,000 illegal abortions each year in Poland since the passage of the tough anti-abortion law, and many women travel abroad on "abortion vacations." In June 2003 there was even a visit by the world's first floating abortion clinic, which docked in Polish ports and then sailed into international waters where women in their tenth week of pregnancy or earlier were given RU-486, a drug that can produce an abortion.[38]

Still, most Polish women wanting an abortion obtain it at home, illegally, and the proliferation of illegal abortions brings its own risks. Illegal abortions in Poland are often carried out in less sanitary conditions than would prevail in hospitals and with less ample resources; the result, as studies conducted during 1999–2000 showed, is an increase in "health and personal problems [for] hundreds of thousands of women in Poland." In addition, there were 31–59 reported cases of infanticide by unwilling mothers annually in the years 1990–99, 20–77 reported cases of child abandonment annually over the same period, and 252–803 children left in hospitals annually in the years 1993–99.[39]

A woman seeking abortion for reasons of rape must obtain a certificate from the prosecutor's office—a certificate not given lightly. The result is that, although some 2,000 rapes are reported annually (the actual number of rapes, including those not reported, may be higher), there were only 53 abortions authorized on grounds of rape in 1998, for example, and in 1999 only one abortion was conducted for reasons of rape.[40] The conclusion is inescapable that the passage of the restrictive law on abortion has not made any appreciable dent in the number of abortions carried out in Poland, but it has affected the health of perhaps hundreds of thousands of women negatively and has resulted in incidents of infanticide, child abandonment, and children being left at hospitals.

Trafficking and forced prostitution. One of the great scandals of the postcommunist systems has been the proliferation of trafficking in women and children, often for the purpose of forcing women into prostitution. Most of the women come from Bulgaria, Romania, Moldova, Russia, Belarus, Ukraine, and Albania, though Polish women have also been trafficked in some numbers. According to the International Organization for Migration (IOM), about 500,000 women are trafficked from formerly communist countries in Eastern Europe to foreign destinations each year.[41] Albanian and other Balkan mafias are knee-deep in trafficking and, according to Italian aid organizations, in 2002 there were perhaps as many as 30,000 young Albanian women working as prostitutes in Western Europe—none of them freely.[42] Some countries are both countries of origin and destination countries—such as Poland and Bosnia. Some women are moved into countries where they do not speak the local language in order to minimize their options, but others are trafficked locally. The women and girls who end up as prostitutes are lured with false promises of a good job in the West and told that they will earn good money and enjoy new opportunities; in some cases, girls have been bartered by their parents for cash; in some cases, invitations to go on vacation have served the purpose; and in yet other cases, the victims have simply been abducted. Once in custody, the woman has no control over her destination or her work. She is escorted to a brothel and then told that her transportation has involved some costs that she must pay back. The woman then ends up working without wages to "repay" the costs of her abduction, with arbitrary fines and dishonest bookkeeping serving to keep the woman in debt for the long term. Even where some women are eventually released from debt, it is "only after months or years of coercive or abusive labor."[43]

Typically, the women's passports are confiscated. If they try to escape and fail, they are beaten severely. If they manage to escape, they find themselves in unfamiliar surroundings, where they often do not speak the local language, lacking personal identification and fearing arrest by local law enforcement authorities. Threats of retaliation against the women's family members back home, in the event of escape, also tend to deter attempts to break out.

The problem of trafficking in women and children is global, and in many countries corrupt officials have actually facilitated trafficking by providing false papers to trafficking agents, turning a blind eye to violations of immigration rules, and taking bribes from the women's employers. Human Rights Watch has also documented many cases in which local police have patronized brothels where trafficked women have been working.[44] Moreover, as Regan Ralph noted in a report presented before a U.S. Senate subcommittee in February 2000,

> Trafficked women may be freed from their employers in police raids, but they are given no access to services or redress and instead face further mistreatment at the hands of authorities. Even when confronted with clear evidence of trafficking and forced labor, officials focus on violations of their immigration regulations and anti-prostitution laws, rather than on violations of the trafficking victims' human rights. Thus, the women are targeted as undocumented migrants and/or prostitutes, and the traffickers either escape entirely, or else face minor penalties for their involvement in illegal migration or businesses of prostitution.[45]

Among the destination countries are Britain, Germany, Austria, Italy, Spain, Greece, Russia, Turkey, Bosnia, and Kosova, where the prostitution racket has boomed, with a sex market located next to the SFOR base in Bihać.[46] Many of the prostitutes working in Bosnia come from Romania, Moldova, and Ukraine. Until public outcry forced the trade underground, many of the women were publicly auctioned off at the so-called Arizona market near Brčko.[47] In late 2001, the U.N. mission in Bosnia-Herzegovina closed down fifteen bars employing women who had been forced into prostitution, and some peacekeepers have been sent home for frequenting local brothels. But on several occasions brothel owners in Bosnia have been tipped off that a police raid was imminent and, by the time the police arrived, the bar had been locked up for the night.[48] In January 2002, authorities in Belgrade announced that some 150 persons had been arrested, most of them on charges related to the trafficking of women; the arrests were the result of a police sweep across more than four hundred bars and nightclubs in various parts of Serbia.[49] Between 2000 and 2004, IOM repatriated more than two thousand trafficked women; but within a year, nearly half of these women had been retrafficked.

EU foreign ministers came to an agreement that combatting human trafficking should be given high priority and, with EU support, the British government drew up proposals including the establishment of a network of special police and immigration officials authorized to share information and coordinate on responses to trafficking. Likewise, the European Commission and the European Parliament have called for systematic action to combat trafficking in human beings.[50] Women's organizations have also demanded that victims of trafficking who give evidence against traffickers be granted asylum, as well as increased penalties for those found guilty of the practice.[51] But where enforcement is concerned, the problem lies in the first place with *local* officials, and that is where the problem must be solved, if it is to be solved at all.

Those most at risk of being lured or abducted into forced prostitution, according to Stana Buchowska, are "young women and girls over the age of 14. These include high school students, trading school students, and college and university students; dropouts from schools; and girls in dormitories, boarding schools, special schools and orphanages. Other high-risk groups are unemployed women and low-waged women."[52]

In March 2005, Helga Konrad, Special Representative in Combating Trafficking in Human Beings (of the Organization for Security and Cooperation in Europe), issued a report accusing European countries of failing to develop a long-term strategy to combat trafficking. Indeed, in 2003 alone some 120,000 women and children "mainly from the Balkans" were trafficked into EU member countries.[53] In the absence of such a strategy, results have been mixed. For example, a report in 2003 cited evidence to suggest that the protection of victims of human trafficking in Bosnia-Herzegovina had improved, while in Moldova, a source of many trafficked women, police broke up a Moldovan-Turkish ring of traffickers in 2005; in Albania, government authorities claimed in January 2006 that there had been a noticeable decrease of trafficking activities in their country. By contrast, as of November 2004, human trafficking was said to be on the rise in Croatia, Serbia, and Bosnia-Herzegovina, and, as of 2005, local authorities reported a rise in human trafficking in Kosovo and Romania.[54]

Domestic violence. Domestic violence and abuse have increased across the region since the collapse of communism. In those areas affected by warfare (Serbia, Croatia, Bosnia), domestic violence has increased most significantly, with one Serbian legislator telling feminist activist Sonja Licht, "Don't talk to me about a law against violence in the family. It would destroy the essence of the Serbian family."[55] In Croatia, a poll conducted in 2000 found that 44.2% of respondents knew at least one woman who had been beaten at home, and 25.8% of respondents said that there were situations in which it was "acceptable" for a husband to beat his wife.[56] As of 2004, domestic violence was said to be increasing in Croatia.[57] About 20% of Slovenian families have had problems with domestic violence,[58] while 85% of divorced women in Poland said that they had been beaten by their husbands (25% said repeatedly, the remaining 60% reported having been beaten at least once).[59] In Romania, the problem became sufficiently serious that, in March 2004, the Ministry of Labor established a National Agency for Family Protection, described as the first agency of its kind in southeast Europe, tasked to assist victims of domestic violence and assist couples engaged in such behavior to break out of the vicious cycle. In Slovakia, the cabinet adopted an action plan to "prevent and eliminate" domestic violence in September 2005, after the Center for the Study of Work and Family released a report (in May 2005) in which it was claimed that 25% of Slovak women are exposed to violence at home.[60]

This problem was discussed in Hungary in early 2006, when Gábor Kuncze, leader of the Free Democrats, and Klára Sándor, a senior official in the same party, called for more effective action to combat domestic violence. According to Sándor, a woman dies of domestic violence in Hungary every week, and the notion that husbands may beat their wives is widespread, tolerated, even accepted in Hungarian society. Moreover, as of 2004 it was not considered a crime in Hungary for a husband to hit his wife. But what is needed, according to Sándor, if the problem is to be eradicated, is nothing less than a kind of "cultural revolution," since the acceptance of violence against women is rooted in "the traditional, stereotypical view of genders, according to which women need paternalistic help in life."[61]

Summary. Since 1989, female representation in political office, including in the national parliaments, has declined; female unemployment has risen; access to abortion has been restricted by law in Poland, resulting in damage to women's health, while recourse to abortion has been stigmatized by conservative religious institutions in other countries; trafficking and forced prostitution have become serious problems; domestic violence has increased; feminism has been demonized and demands for gender equality ridiculed; conservative forces have done their best to revive traditional gender models in which women are subordinated to men; and the general quality of life has declined. Given all of these conditions, the conclusion seems inescapable to me that the situation of women in Eastern Europe has tangibly deteriorated since the collapse of communism.

THE BROADER CONTEXT

The restoration of the traditional family—an impossible goal actually, though of no less interest to conservatives for all that—is associated with a revival of homophobic and transophobic prejudices. Conservatives want to depict those who reject the traditional authority of husbands over wives as sinners (or traitors), to draw firm boundaries, and to exclude those who violate those boundaries from the "communion of saints." As R. I. Moore showed in his study of the Catholic Church in eleventh- and twelfth-century Europe, the creation of out-groups disciplined those fearful of being ostracized, forcing them to conform to the (new) rules being imposed on the society.[62] Not surprisingly, Orthodox, Catholic, and certain other Christian communities have been in the forefront of the new homophobia in Eastern Europe, though other groups (especially nationalists) have embraced sexual intolerance as well. Examining Tudjman-era Croatia, Tatjana Pavlović writes:

> Both Serbs and homosexuals "betray" the Nation. Ethnic and sexual scapegoating go hand in hand and are justified by imaginary, arbitrary borders. The homosexual/Serb exemplifies the creation, reification, and expulsion of the Other. It is an undesirable element in both family and national rhetoric. On the level of the family, the homosexual is a dark counterpart of the hypermasculine father/defender/warrior.[63]

Although the Roman Catholic Church has blocked the recognition of gay and lesbian marriage in Poland and sought to keep neutral treatments of homosexuality off the airwaves, the Orthodox Church has been far more energetic in its campaign against affection between members of the same sex. The Orthodox Church's position is that all sexual contacts not serving the purpose of procreation are sinful; since same-sex relations cannot lead to procreation, it follows, for that organization, that they are sinful.[64] The Russian Orthodox Church threatened to resign from the World Council of Churches in 1999 when that body authorized a study of sexual diversity with an eye to reassessing its posture on homosexuality, and clergy of the Serbian Orthodox Church have been associated with expressions of intolerance against gays and lesbians—in the case of Father Žarko Gavrilović, a retired Serbian priest, with a group of skinheads who attacked a small group of gay Serbs who were trying to stage the country's first gay pride march in June 2001.

But it is the Romanian Orthodox Church that has found itself at the vortex of the battle against homosexuality. The church had made its peace with Romanian dictator Nicolae Ceauşescu, who in 1968 had toughened the anti-gay legislation in his country. But when Ceauşescu fell from power, Romania sought entry into the Council of Europe, and in 1993 was admitted on the condition that it change eleven of its laws, among them the law affecting homosexuality, to conform with European standards. The Romanian Orthodox Church was unbudgingly opposed to the proposed decriminalization of homosexuality, however, and held to its line that homosexuality was a sin and that practicing homosexuals should go to prison. Patriarch Teoctist, who in his youth had been a member of the fascistic Iron Guard, even tried to persuade the country's parliament that the Council of Europe was not really serious about its demand that Romania repeal its anti-gay legislation and would admit Romania even if the law remained.[65] After an eight-year battle, the parliament finally voted to agree to the Council's conditions and repealed the anti-gay legislation.

The phenomenon of Christian intolerance is well known; moreover, according to psychologists, hatred of designated out-groups "may give rise to highly pleasurable aggressive behaviors . . . rationalized as an expression of righteous indignation."[66] The "recreational" aspect of gay beating is confirmed by Martha Nussbaum, who notes, based on research in the American and Canadian context, that anti-gay violence is often motivated in the first place by a desire to escape boredom and have some "fun."[67] But where Christian intolerance is concerned, it is not without guile. Its ostensible irrationality is cunning, as revealed in its effort to pass itself off as Christian love. Its cunning lies precisely in its utility in maintaining clear gender boundaries and clear gender roles, revealing once again the centrality of sexuality for religious ethics. Against the tendency of some religious organizations to limit women's prerogatives, to legitimate violent acts against women who dare to deviate from prescribed religious norms, and to countenance hate speech against nonconformists, Nussbaum has urged that "there is a basic core of international morality" that all religious organizations must respect.[68]

RIVAL CULTURES

Four rival cultures are clashing in Eastern Europe—liberalism, nationalism, conservative Christianity, and feminism. Although there have been efforts to marry liberalism and nationalism and others to conjoin Christianity and feminism, these pairs are not natural allies. Nationalism and conservative Christianity are long-standing allies, on the other hand, and the compatibility of the left wing of the liberal tradition with feminism can be traced back to John Stuart Mill's *Subjection of Women*.[69] But, although liberalism may be interpreted in such a way as to imply and entail feminism, the concerns of feminism go beyond those of liberalism in a crucial respect. While both liberalism and feminism emphasize the importance of human rights, tolerance, and equality, feminists have been more inclined to stress the importance of cultural change (as per textbooks) than liberals, and more inclined to support the use of quotas and affirmative action programs to redress imbalance.

Classical liberalism has been strong on defining individual rights, on demarcating the imperative of the harm principle, and on establishing the necessity for the state to be confessionally neutral. At least some segments of the liberal tradition have also been strong in defining moral imperatives under Natural Law. The liberal tradition has been weaker in defining any imperative for human solidarity or in according any recognition of animal rights or even species rights (along the lines of the rights of a species to survive) or in mandating conditions for the preservation of the environment or in prescribing active remedies to assure equality between the sexes. Among the reasons for this weakness are the fact that the main lines of liberalism were developed in the eighteenth century, under entirely different conditions and within a culture facing very different challenges from those faced today; and the fact that the liberal tradition was influenced by the "realist" notions of the illiberal Thomas Hobbes and associated with the laissez-faire prescriptions of Adam Smith and his successors, with the result that sectors of the liberal tradition were drawn into the realm of social Darwinism. A full embrace of the equality of women, of animal rights, of the duty of states to protect the environment and assure a decent living to all their citizens and legal residents, and of the place of solidarist thinking in economic life does not represent a repudiation of the liberal tradition but an expansion of it, moving it, as it were, to the next level.

Finally, where democracy is concerned, the way the concept has increasingly come to be operationalized—emphasizing elections rather than participation; passing off short terms as the best guarantee of responsible government even at the risk that officeholders, fearing the loss of their seats, will feel the need to pander to the public rather than defend the public's best interests; paying too little attention to the need for the public to be informed about public issues; and allowing entirely unqualified persons to run for public office and be elected, even inflicting serious damage on the public interest—has undermined the very principles supposedly being furthered by what we have come to call democracy. As David Hollenbach has warned, the neoliberal tendency to trust to the struggle among competing interest groups to produce a result satisfactory for society as a whole subverts the democratic project itself insofar as "interest group politics is frequently incapable of even naming the social bonds that increasingly destine us to sharing either a common good or a 'common bad.'"[70] Where solidarity is weak, where women are unable to participate in the political system on an equal basis, and where participation itself is too often reduced to marking a box on a ballot every four years, democracy itself is attenuated.

CONCLUSION

When I was still teaching in the United States, I would hear American students tell me, from time to time, that they objected in principle to any system providing rewards, recognition, and promotion on the basis of merit; since the system of grading itself is based on merit, this attitude struck me as shocking, especially in view of the fact that the alternatives—corruption, cliques, favoritism, nepotism, and outright criminality—are generally considered to be corrosive of civilized society. But in registering this "opinion," the students were, perhaps unconsciously, merely registering their acceptance of and resignation to some of the negative features of the system in which they found themselves living. Against this conservative posture of resignation, liberals demand equality, only to bicker about whether equality should be merely an equality under the law, an equality of opportunity, or an equality of result. What feminists have wanted is to cut through the Gordian knot of weak-kneed professions of egalitarianism and "to change the economic system to one more based on merit."[71] The advantages of meritocratic criteria over criteria derived from favoritism, nepotism, male bonding, corruption, or the perverse resentment of merit that results in the rewarding of the mediocre and the punishment of the talented would seem to be so obvious as not to require demonstration. Indeed, so obvious are these advantages that those promoting or differentially rewarding the undeserving always attempt to make the claim that the undeserving are, in fact, deserving. Meritocracy cuts through the self-serving lies and constitutes not only the point at which feminism and liberalism come together but also a vital demonstration of the way the feminist agenda serves the interests of all persons.

A vision of a better world can start with Vladimir Tismaneanu's demand that a community be based on truth, trust, and tolerance.[72] More concretely, a better world—whether in Eastern Europe or elsewhere—must, of necessity, involve provisions for good schools, affordable access to job training, assured low-cost medical and therapeutic care at a fixed level of quality, and sufficient economic opportunities. Also essential are the marginalization of discourses of intolerance, whether justified on the basis of religion or on some other basis, the vigorous investigation and prosecution of traffickers and those involved in the sex slavery racket, and provisions for the adequate rehabilitation of victims of trafficking, and—I would add—the use of sensible quota systems to assure a reasonable approximation to gender equality and the decriminalization of moral choices in areas where widespread consensus does not exist (e.g., in the area of abortion).

These elements are the minimal ingredients with which all members of society have the real possibility to develop their talents and feel that they are valued members of society. But it is no accident that so-called realists talk endlessly, not about building good schools or providing low-cost medical care, but about law and order—and that without ever being able to achieve it. It is precisely the failure of realists to understand that civil peace is the by-product, not of coercion, but of strategies of policymaking directed toward fostering a sense of community that has accounted for the failure of many a realist scheme in the past.[73]

It is also time to demand an expansion of liberal theory to embrace the rights of species to survive, the individual rights of all living beings from reptiles to fish to birds to mammals, and the right of all of us to require that our governments take drastic measures to combat global warming (even as some scientists already tell us that the process is now irreversible) and to save the planet from extinction. In defining species rights, moreover, if there is a right to survive, then species (all species) have a right to the preservation of the natural habitats in which they can live. The notion that humankind enjoys some special right to destroy itself and the entire planet does not impress me as a right that can withstand scrutiny. Survival is the prerequisite to the enjoyment of all other rights, and it is absurd that politicians prattle about law and order or about the right to own firearms while failing to address the most pressing challenge of our generation.

Although the recent conflicts in the western Balkans have highlighted the importance of a sense of community, the success or failure of the transition from communism to a legitimate system of governance and a healthy society depends on a variety of other factors too, including success in the fight against organized crime and political corruption, the struggle against poverty, the development of functioning democratic institutions, and the assurance of procedural regularity in the system and full respect for women. As long as these challenges are not met, no transition in the region can be counted as a success.

8

THE PURPOSE OF POLITICAL ASSOCIATION

 t has become less fashionable of late to pose the big question, almost as if it should be seen as somehow in bad taste to ask about purposes and ultimate ends. And yet, if one has no answer to the question—What is the purpose of political association?—then perhaps one is navigating without a map. The great philosophers—Plato, Aristotle, Bodin, Hobbes, Hooker, Locke, Kant, and Hegel—all had answers to this question. But today, when political association appears as a given, and when even voluntary associations tend to emerge when preexisting states fail, as manifested in the declaration of dissociation by Slovenia in June 1991, the question can hardly be avoided. But the question about the purpose of political association is not an ontological question or a question based on the postulation of a "state of nature." It is, rather, a question that directs us to the standards to which we are prepared to hold our regimes and which will serve as the measure of those regimes' performance.

With that understanding, I offer that the purpose of political association is to provide a secure setting in which people, both collectively and individually, can develop morally, culturally, socially, and technologically in cooperation with each other, minimizing hurt to each other or to other living beings, and can protect and safeguard individual and communal rights as well as the resources, both human and natural, upon which the continued survival and prosperity of the community and the survival of the ecosphere depend. This answer includes the values of (long-term) survival, security for people, moral, cultural, and technological development, the interests of both the community and the individual, and protection for both individual and communal rights, such as the right of the community to adequate low-cost public education and medical care. The assurance of low-cost education, low-cost medical care, and sufficient security so that people's routine decisions and activities are not constrained by fear of each other is essential to assure real freedom, since a talented young person who is unable to obtain an education sufficient to realize her full potential is no more free to pursue her dream, for example, than is someone bankrupted by medical bills.

This answer has some resonance with the political thought of several thinkers, including Richard Hooker (who laid special stress on the role of the state in fostering moral development), John Stuart Mill (who wanted the state to assure liberty for all, so that civilization might continue to advance), and Tom Paine (who stressed the importance of assuring financial security for society's residents), as well as Catholic social thought (in which communal interests are also taken into account, alongside those of individuals). The answer has the advantage over some other proposed answers in that it underlines the need to safeguard natural resources, in order to maximize the interests of the community over the long term, and in that, by omitting the protection of property, it does not lend itself to subversion for the purpose of protecting the rich against the poor. At the same time, the stress on securing the possibility for people to develop morally, culturally, socially, and technologically presumes and entails guarantees for individual rights as well as the rights of the community.

In 1989–90, when the communist organizational monopoly in Eastern Europe collapsed, the question about the purposes of political association was reopened. The answers that were found reflected the problems perceived to have emerged and the interests of those in positions of power. Thus, in the German Democratic Republic, the question became a question about national reunification (who should associate with whom?), while in the decaying Socialist Federated Republic of Yugoslavia the question was rather the reverse, namely, who had the right to reject association with whom? In Poland, the Catholic Church read the question as involving values and answered that the purpose of political association is to protect the nation's values, which were said to be Catholic values. At various levels of all of these societies, there were those who wanted to read the purpose of association in terms of the possibility for enterprising persons, whether honest or dishonest, to get rich. What is striking about these answers is that they all reflect the perspectives or interests of specific strata in these societies, be it some minority of people or the majority; in none of the societies of Eastern Europe could one find loud voices stressing survivability or the safe-guarding of resources.

WHAT KIND OF FREEDOM?
WHAT KIND OF DEMOCRACY?

The revolutions of 1989–90 were about freedom—ask anyone in the region. But what kind of freedom? Americans, in particular, tend to equate free-dom with those freedoms for which the generation of 1776 fought: freedom of speech, assembly, religion, and, for some, gun ownership, as well as free-dom from taxation without representation. But these were not the free-doms I heard people talk about in the German Democratic Republic (GDR), when I visited there in summer 1988. Instead, people talked about wanting the freedom to travel where they liked and the freedom to pur-chase such consumer goods as they wanted. Freedom of religion? There were restrictions, of course, but there was considerable variation across the region. In the GDR, for example, the largest religious body, the Evangeli-cal (Lutheran) Church, had reached a modus vivendi with the regime be-ginning in 1978, under the motto "Church in Socialism," and since then had been able to build church facilities in hitherto churchless cities, to broad-cast the liturgy, and to enjoy other prerogatives while continuing to operate departments of theology *within* the state universities. Moreover, the fact that certain religious groups, such as the Christian Scientists, Nazarenes, and Hare Krishna, were banned scarcely troubled the Evangelical Church or the Catholic Church, which were thereby relieved of potential compe-tition from those quarters. The GDR was, of course, an extreme example— yet not without some similarities to Poland, Croatia, and even Hungary. Only in Romania did the popular uprising against communist authorities— and there was a genuine uprising in Romania—have a clear connection with religion, and even there the focus was on the regime's intention to transfer a popular pastor from his parish rather than on freedom of religion as such.

Censorship, on the other hand, was more of a problem, especially in those states, such as the GDR and Yugoslavia, that operated on the basis of post-publication censorship. In these states, when church newspapers were suppressed, it was after the church had already spent money producing the issues in question, and it was both too late and too expensive to print a fresh issue for the given week. In other states, such as Poland, Czechoslovakia, Romania, and Bulgaria, pre-publication censorship was the order of the day, and editors had to submit articles and layouts to the censors for approval before going into production. Where church newspapers were concerned, this had the advantage (over post-publication censorship) that the church did not end up having entire issues confiscated and suppressed, and there could also be some room for negotiation with a censor. On the other hand, entire paragraphs or even articles might be axed and, in Czechoslovakia, Romania, and Bulgaria, communist authorities could contribute articles to local "church" newspapers such as *Katolické noviny* and *Romanian Church News* (the latter being published in English).

Freedom from surveillance was also a high priority, and this was generally associated with a desire to see the publication of the names of informers and the formulation of some form of revenge against those who had collaborated with the regime in this way. Freedom of movement within the country, freedom to change jobs, and freedom to avoid politics (e.g., by not voting) were also prized; communist regimes had typically demanded 100% participation in elections, thereby forcing their citizens to endorse the single-candidate slate. For intellectuals, freedom of inquiry, freedom to choose their topics of research, and freedom to publish articles that did not require self-censorship were also valued; scholars in communist Czechoslovakia had been effectively prevented from conducting research on medieval topics, and in the GDR scholars interested in Martin Luther or Thomas Müntzer had to follow the party line, which, in the case of Luther, changed over the years. Only after all of these other desired freedoms are mentioned can one speak of the desire for freedom of political association.

And there were other passions driving the revolutions of 1989. There was resentment against an anti-meritocratic system that blended privilege for party cadres with a rigid egalitarianism for the rest of society, crushing initiative and incentive alike to the extent that the Czechoslovak "Action Program" of 1968 could claim that the system gave "careless, idle, and irresponsible people an advantage over dedicated and diligent workers, the unqualified over the qualified, the technically backward over the talented and initiative-oriented."[1] There was resentment among all those who had lost careers or loved ones or property as a result of communist repression. There was resentment at the way history had been rewritten by the communists and a strong desire to produce new histories to displace the communist versions of history. And, perhaps above all, there was a naïve faith that democracy—whatever that might mean—would prove to be not only a fairer system but even some sort of elysium, where dreams could come true.

But what kind of democracy should it be? The menu is long, with some potentially overlapping dishes. Having repudiated socialist democracy, as it was called, locals were not at all tempted by restributive democracy or what has come to be called consultative democracy, with its suggestion of authoritarian rulers consulting people only when forced by circumstances to do so. But was liberal democracy the best option or would clerical democracy (whose conservative Christian advocates in Poland were discussed in chapter 6) be preferable, as some right-wing parties have urged, albeit without using that expression. Where a liberal democracy or laic state enshrines the separation of church and state and emphasizes tolerance and respect for the harm principle, advocates of clerical democracy prefer to see state legislation molded by the dominant religious establishment's moral agenda and offer interpretations of tolerance and the harm principle consistent with that agenda. So, for example, where liberal democrats want to see sexual minorities protected under law from persecution or discrimination, believing that harm to members of sexual minorities should be avoided as far as possible, clerical democrats argue that the mere presence of sexual minorities does some sort of harm to heterosexuals, who need to be protected from gays and lesbians, transsexuals and transvestites, by being allowed to discriminate against them in jobs, housing, and education.

Then there are the advocates of national democracy (see chapter 7), who want to marry democracy to one or another form of nationalism. Where the hybrid "liberal nationalism" is concerned, the final result depends on whether the hybrid is tilted more to the liberal side or more to the national side of the equation. But in the case of illiberal nationalism, such as one finds in Serbia even today, the resulting national democracy takes the form of resentment of neighboring states and peoples, intolerance, and the rehabilitation of the Axis-collaborationist Chetniks of World War II.[2] Such nationalist democracy distorts the social agenda by focusing society's energy on past struggles and on resentments against neighbors rather than on such tasks as can lead to a better life for those living in the country.

THE NATURE OF THE STATE

To ask about the purpose of political association is also, by implication, to ask about the purpose of the state, insofar as the state is the vehicle for political association. Various answers have been given to this question over the past two and a half millennia. These answers have generally been thought to have a broad, if not transhistorical, validity, but typically they are formulated with an eye to the problems of the age. Thus Hobbes, writing at the time of the English civil war, emphasized the state's role in assuring civil peace, while Locke, as already noted, underlined that the state should protect property. In the twenty-first century, the present dangers, to which any philosophy of the state must respond, include environmental threats (destruction of habitats, extinction of species, pollution, climate change), economic dangers (the rise of global mega-corporations, the widening gulf between the super-rich and the super-indigent), overpopulation, threats to human dignity (including those outlined in the previous chapter), and the dual processes of cultural homogenization and the commercialization of popular culture, which change the role of popular culture in society by downplaying local traditions and deflating its earlier political engagement (as seen in protest rock, for example) and by emphasizing pop culture's function as entertainment.

These processes threaten all societies, but the threat is differentiated. In the United States, for example, the environmental and economic threats are arguably the most salient, while the question of overpopulation does not yet present itself as a problem. Environmental and economic dangers are also present in Eastern Europe, together with the penetration of American cultural artifacts and the accompanying processes of homogenization and commercialization of popular culture.[3] The escalating deterioration of environmental quality has not only sparked scattered ecoterrorist initiatives, in which real estate development is targeted for destruction in the interest of saving plant life and habitats, but also inspired a concept of "environmental democracy." Robyn Eckersley defines environmental democracy as "a 'democracy-for-the-affected,' since the class of beings entitled to moral consideration in democratic deliberation (whether infants, the infirm, the yet-to-be-born, or non-human species) will invariably be wider than the class of those who are actually alive and physically and intellectually capable of engaging in democratic deliberation."[4] Eckersley's concept is reminiscent of Kant's suggestion that, whereas humans have both rights and duties, nonhuman species have rights only, and points to a concept of democracy as a form of government that might aspire to defending the interests of animals as well as humans. This, in turn, suggests a distinction between the representation of (human) citizens and the representation *of the interests* of nonhuman species but, as Amy Gutmann and Dennis Thompson suggest, even the most principled formula of representation evokes the twin dangers of elitism and populism, which they define as "the tendency of representatives to pander to their constituents."[5]

If we understand democratic government in terms of representation, then we may ask who, in practice, is being represented. In "old democracies," political parties have existed for so long that their origins as the advocates of specific interests have become obscured—though Hartmut Krauss reported that in the United States the Christian Coalition enjoyed the dominant influence in the Republican Party in at least twelve states by the turn of the century.[6] Whether or not the Republican Party is a clerical party, there are certainly examples of clerical parties in Eastern Europe, with the League of Polish Families serving as an apt example.

If political parties may represent ecclesiastical interests and perspectives, they may also represent corporate interests. In Ukraine, for example, large, formerly state-owned enterprises were, by the mid-1990s, divided among three regionally defined clans of industrial elites, each throwing up its own political party to advance its own economic interests.[7] Or again, in Serbia, political parties were generated by agencies and power blocs existing within the establishment itself, so that the parties may be said to have emerged as engines of representation of the interests of those agencies and blocs, as if the purpose of representation was to allow government to be represented in government.[8] In Kosovo and Macedonia, political parties have been founded by insurgents, so that they might continue to struggle, in a parliamentary forum, for the same objectives for which they had fought with arms.

The classic model of Millian democracy is perhaps most closely approached in Slovenia, Croatia, and Hungary, where groups of intellectuals set up political parties in order to challenge the Communist Party and advocate values such as freedom of speech and freedom of religion. Bianca Adair argues that one reason for Hungary's relatively successful democratization is precisely that the process was initiated by technocrats and intellectuals—a factor that made for political stability.[9] In all of these countries, moreover, the Communist Party itself gave birth to a new political party, usually with a transformed program, while in Slovenia the old transmission belt, the League of Socialist Youth, gave birth to the Liberal Democratic Party, which dominated Slovenian politics for more than a decade (1992–2004). The ways in which the political parties of Eastern Europe emerged are, thus, as diverse as the interests they represent.

THE EUROPEAN UNION AND THE
TRANSFORMATION OF DEMOCRACY

In the United States, there have been expressions of concern that the civic engagement of American citizens may have dipped to an all-time low.[10] But, although it is true that traditional civic associations and forms of civic engagement have paled, in the United States at least, evangelical organizations such as the Christian Right, Focus on the Family, and the National Right to Life Committee have filled the void.[11] And just as traditional civic associations aspired to defend particular concepts of the common good, so too do clerical associations (and parties) aspire to defend particular concepts of the common good, even if some persons, such as unwed, pregnant women and members of sexual minorities may feel excluded from and even victimized by this clerical vision of the common good. But for clericals, as for evangelist Jonathan Blanchard (in his Oberlin College address of 1839), "society is perfect where what is right in theory exists in fact; where practice coincides with principle, and the Law of God is the Law of the Land."[12]

Across Eastern Europe there is a revival of civic engagement, though that revival is uneven. As of 1999, the percentage of people who belonged to at least one voluntary association ranged from a low of 9.6% in Romania to a high of 47% in Slovakia. Ranked in between were Poland (12.4%), Bulgaria (13.7%), Hungary (14.6%), Croatia (21.5%), Slovenia (27%), and the Czech Republic (30.8%).[13] But it is the religious establishments that have flexed their muscles in areas they deem to be of high priority: abortion, homosexuality, respect for Christian values, prayer in the schools, school textbooks (including about sex education), and the like. Churches have not, of course, been major players in foreign policy or in debates about privatization or in any of a number of other issues including environmental protection, housing, or public transport, although local bishops have occasionally spoken out on the subject of corruption.[14]

Enter the European Union. For the postcommunist states of Eastern Europe, the prospect of membership in the Council of Europe and the European Union has exerted great attraction and conduced the governments to agree to adapt legislation to accord with EU guidelines. In Slovakia, for example, in response to EU pressure the government adopted legislation to permit greater use of Hungarian and Romany in public life.[15] In Romania, pressure from the Council of Europe resulted in the decriminalization of homosexuality, in the face of desperate resistance on the part of the Romanian Orthodox Church.[16] But it was the draft EU constitution that mobilized the Catholic and Orthodox establishments, pitting their vision of the union as a "spiritual" union against the drafters' vision of a union inspired by liberal values. What the Catholics and Orthodox had in mind specifically was that God should be mentioned in the preamble to the constitution, that the continent's Christian heritage be mentioned in the constitution, and that there be specific guarantees to countries requesting it that there would never be any pressure on them to legalize abortion (Poland being a signal case here).[17]

Valéry Giscard d'Estaing was appointed to chair the Presidium of the Convention on the Future of Europe, which was tasked to draft a constitution for the European Union by April 2003; after the preamble and the first sixteen articles of the draft constitution were published, controversy flared. Orthodox bishops convened an inter-Orthodox conference in Heraklion, Crete, on March 18–19, 2003 to review the constitutional charter and to draw up recommendations for its revision. Chaired by His Holiness Bartholomew, Patriarch of Constantinople, the conference reached an agreement on six points, recommending that the EU constitutional charter incorporate Christian values, recognize the principles of "Christian, Biblical, Greek and Roman ancient heritage," protect not only the individual rights of people but also their collective rights, ensure "the right of all the traditional European Churches and religions" (presumably to advance their social agendas through government legislation), include provisions for the regulation of relations between church and state, and "set clearly specified criteria that would stipulate a clear attitude toward sects and proselytism."[18] Subsequently, in June 2003, Archbishop Christodoulos assailed the European Union for having omitted a reference to God or the Christian heritage in the draft constitution and complained that those who had drafted the charter were "*expelling* Christianity from the constitution of the European Union."[19]

In Poland, the Catholic Church apparently nurtured fears that the European Union would promote not only "secularism" but also homosexuality and pornography. In March 2002 the Polish episcopate sent an official statement to the president, the prime minister, the Vatican, and the European Convention, underlining, as Archbishop Henryk Muszyński put it, that "the Church regards the EU as a community of the spirit" and that "according to the Church, Europe is above all an entity of the spirit and of certain values."[20] In May of that same year, Cardinal Glemp and President Kwaśniewski issued a joint statement calling on the European Union to include a reference to Europe's Christian tradition in the eventual EU constitution. A spokesperson for the episcopate offered the suggestion that the Polish constitution could serve as a model for the EU constitution in this regard.[21]

COMPETING VISIONS

I suggested earlier that liberalism be understood as a syndrome consisting of rule of law, individual rights (and duties), tolerance, respect for the harm principle, equality, and neutrality of the state in matters of religion. Clericalism, as the advocacy that the parameters of state be defined in accordance with divine law, rejects the appeal to state neutrality in matters of religion outright. But clericalism defines each of the other elements in a way that differs significantly from the liberal interpretation. Tolerance, for example, is limited to speech and behavior considered to be within the limits set by divine law, and the harm principle is expanded to include a notion of spiritual harm, so that a Christian heterosexual may claim to be harmed by the mere presence of a gay or lesbian person in the vicinity. In this and other ways, clericalism has systematic points of difference with liberalism.

Clerical democracy is only one alternative to liberal democracy. Another alternative with advocates in Eastern Europe is what I call *national democracy,* by which I mean democracy "of the nation, by the nation, and for the nation." What, then, is "the nation"? It is the dominant nationality in any given state. This means that national democracy, as I have defined it, is intended to exclude or discriminate against unwanted minorities. Its modus operandi is not the liberal emphasis on individual rights (and, for left-liberals, also communal rights) but the claim that so-called national rights may trump individual rights. If, following Michael Emerson, we understand a "racialized society" as one in which "society's goods . . . [are allocated] unequally along racial lines" and in which "race matters considerably for who people are, whom they know, and what their chances in life are,"[22] then, by extension, we may understand a national democracy as a system in which political rights are allocated unequally along national lines and in which language and ascribed nationality matter considerably for who people think they are, who others think people are, and what their chances in life are. National democracy, as I have defined it here, has had its champions in most, if not all, of the countries of Eastern Europe and, provided that one is prepared to use the term "democracy" loosely, may be said to have been the dominant form of government in Milošević's Serbia, Tudjman's Croatia, and Mečiar's Slovakia.

To my way of thinking, clerical democracy and national democracy have more in common with each other than either does with liberal democracy. For liberal democrats, to the extent that there is a concept of sin—though the word would never be used—it would be associated, in the first place, with intolerance and with willful harm to others, especially at an individual level; harm to the environment is somehow neglected by some well-meaning liberal democrats, in spite of its damage to human communities and nonhuman habitats. The classical liberal democratic project is, moreover, inclusive, in the sense that it aspires to put all citizens on an equal footing, respecting their diverse cultures and religious traditions, and to base the law on a concept of reasonableness, with parties to legislative debate expected to provide, on request, reasons for their policy preferences.[23] Such reasons would need to include a justification of proposed policies in terms of their impact on the lives of permanent residents of the country, whether citizens or not.

For clerical democrats and national democrats, by contrast, the purpose of political association is not to put all citizens on an equal footing, let alone to respect their diverse cultures and religious traditions, but, on the contrary, to find a common denominator to which all "should" agree. The controversy about prayer in the schools in the United States is illustrative of the point. While it may, perhaps, be possible to find a prayer formulation that could be more or less acceptable to all Christians—although I am skeptical of that—any Christian prayer immediately sends a signal to Jews, Muslims, Buddhists, Hindus, Theosophists, and members of other religious traditions represented in the United States that they are second-class citizens, that their prayers are not the prayers "of the nation," that their cultures are subordinate, not equal, to the Christian tradition. This is precisely why James Madison fought so hard against ecclesiastical establishment in the United States. Where legislative debates are concerned, clericals and nationalists provide entirely different reasons—either referring matters to God's law, as they understand it, or basing their preferences on "blood and soil," race, language purity, or nationality.

Insofar as the systems of Eastern Europe serve as arenas for rivalry among the advocates of liberal democracy, clerical democracy, and national democracy, we may understand these variations on the theme of democracy as competing programs, whose advocates aspire to shape the systems in which they operate. They are the programs of specific actors, who are engaged in competition over values, among other things. A final alternative to be discussed here is pragmatic democracy, by which I mean a democratic

vision inspired by notions compatible with those of the self-declared prag-
matist Richard Rorty. Where liberals, clericals, and nationalists all subscribe
to one or another notion of rights, understood to be transcendent or transhistorical, Rorty, who cites John Dewey as a particular inspiration, denies
that there are "universal principles of rationality" or any moral universals
and describes pragmatism as seeking to maximize variety and freedom.[24]

For Rorty, moral codes are "mostly a matter of historical narratives (including scenarios about what is likely to happen in certain future contin-
gencies), rather than of philosophical metanarratives." He resists any form
of transcendent authority and, in this spirit, says that he looks forward to "a
time when the notions of Divine Will and of Cognitive Command have . . .
been replaced by that of A Free Consensus of Enquirers." Until that time,
he promises to content himself with "point[ing] to the seeming futility of
metaphysical activity."[25]

This looks very open ended and very subjective, even if the notion of
a consensus suggests a collective subjectivity. Rorty's pragmatism is, in fact,
aimed at the Kantian tradition above all; indeed, in *Consequences of Pragmatism,* Rorty even suggests, in reference to a list of "morally praiseworthy
actions," that he "doubt[s] that there is anything general and useful to say
about what makes them all good."[26] That is to say, he denies that there is any
principle (such as the categorical imperative) or appeal to reason (as per
Natural Law) or reference to consequences (as per Bentham's "greatest
good for the greatest number") to which one might appeal in justifying why
one calls one action good and another bad. Rather, insofar as he refers moral
norms to the "free consensus" of locals, Rorty offers subjectivity, or better,
personal opinion, as the bellweather of right and wrong. This, in turn, has
the consequence that, if traditions differ radically from one society to another, morality may differ to the same extent from one society to the next.
This understanding may help us to understand Saudi practices of chopping
the hands off pickpockets or Islamic practices of veiling, but it does not
seem to provide any clue as to what to make of such things as mass rape or
genocide. I doubt very much that Rorty wants us to think that these depend
on local understandings, and if he would allow that there are indeed some
universals in morality, then, as far as I can see, his protests against Habermas[27] go up in smoke.

But there is a problem with abandoning any firm standards of right
and wrong, namely, that without such standards there is no foundation for
any firm notion of human rights. The nineteenth-century German school-
teacher Max Stirner, ill famed for his nihilistic *Ego and His Own* (1844),

made a similar case 150 years earlier, ending up denying that even freedom was a guiding principle for him (since he was against all principles) and basing claims not on what was right but on what he wanted. A "pragmatic democracy" à la Rorty would be motivated, as we have seen, by the quest to maximize variety (of choices) and freedom (of individuals) and would appear to involve mechanisms of deliberative democracy but, lacking any framework for establishing normative standards, would not be able to generate motivations in the moral field aside from self-interest. While Rorty per se may not have inspired a widespread following in Eastern Europe, the skepticism he expresses concerning metaphysical concepts such as Natural Law is not unknown in the region. As such, his ideas are relevant to this discussion.

CONCLUSION

In chapter 7, I outlined four competing currents in Eastern Europe: liberalism, conservative Christianity (i.e., clericalism), nationalism, and feminism. The rival visions of democracy described in this chapter—liberal, clerical, national, and pragmatic—overlap only in part with the currents identified in the previous chapter. Feminism was not treated in this chapter because, as I have already indicated, in my view feminism is best seen as the fulfillment and culmination of classical liberalism. The visions outlined in this chapter differ not in terms of procedural preferences but in terms of their values and cognitive frameworks. Liberals and pragmatists lay more stress on individual rights than do clericals and nationalists, though Kant gives more credence to individual autonomy than does Rorty. Classical liberals and clericals stress a transcendent moral law (Natural Law for the classical liberals, divine law for the clericals), while nationalists and pragmatists emphasize collective subjectivity. Liberals and pragmatists are necessarily secular in orientation, while nationalists may be secular or clerically inclined. Liberals, nationalists, and pragmatists are all inclined to talk about freedom, though for nationalists the concern is for the freedom of the nation, while clericals place their emphasis on spiritual truth. Variety (i.e., pluralism) is a value for liberals and pragmatists but potentially problematic for nationalists and clericals. Tolerance is a virtue for both liberals and pragmatists— for liberals as a matter of principle, for pragmatists because tolerance is a prerequisite for both variety and freedom; tolerance is seriously circumscribed for both clericals and nationalists. And finally, whereas clericalism and nationalism both may assume a utopian form, liberalism and pragmatism are clearly anti-utopian in orientation.

On the face of it, liberalism and pragmatism would seem to have more in common with each other than with either nationalism or clericalism. But, at the same time, it should be clear that what we are dealing with is four competing visions, each with its own potential constituency, each offering discrete benefits, and each involving certain costs. And while I have suggested that classical liberalism may offer the surest guarantee of a legitimate system, that suggestion is premised on the supposition that classical liberalism stands the best chance of winning general assent. When such assent is lacking, an alternative vision may prevail, as the Chetnik nationalist vision seems to be prevailing in post-Milošević Serbia. Whether such a vision can pass the test of time is, however, another question.

9

LEGITIMACY OR ORDER
Which Is the Fulcrum?

Make no mistake: both liberal idealists and liberal realists value legitimacy and order.[1] The difference is that, where idealists believe that civic order is a consequence of system legitimacy and that legitimacy is, in turn, measured in terms of the system's harmony with certain values and norms, realists construe legitimacy as but the face of civil order, however achieved. Machiavelli, still a central reference point for the realist tradition, or what's left of it,[2] had no objection to legitimacy as such but placed his emphasis on the *appearance* of legitimacy or, rather, on the appearance of personal virtue on the part of the ruler, which he, not being an idealist, equated with legitimacy.

It is worth remembering that Samuel P. Huntington, the dean among contemporary realists, treated democracy and Leninism, in his *Political Order in Changing Societies* (1968), as functionally equivalent, insofar as they both assured (so he wrote) civil order. It is this function-mindedness of realism that accounts for the fact that Huntington treated the communist systems as functionally equivalent to Western democracies in terms of expected stability, imperviousness to collapse and/or revolution, and life expectancy. Realists at times expressed contempt for those (idealists), such as Vladimir Tismaneanu,[3] who were engaged in research into values and dissent, human rights movements, women's organizations, and other agents promoting concepts of civil society, because these realists were skeptical about the impact norms and values could have in the world of politics. They dismissed or ignored predictions of the eventual collapse of communism registered from 1980 onward by such observers as Ernst Kux, George Schöpflin, Anneli Ute Gabanyi, Ivan Volgyes, and Dimitry Pospielovsky as mere wishful thinking and insisted that communism would last "forever."[4] They ignored the dramatic findings by "Marta Toch" (a pen name) concerning the growth of an independent civil society in Poland in the early 1980s, which she called a "quiet revolution" and documented in a 101-page report released at the end of 1986.[5] And when proven wrong, completely wrong, rather than abandoning the realist paradigm, with its equation of democratic stability with the putative legitimacy of Leninist systems, they preferred to imagine variously either that *everyone* is a realist or that the predictive powers of realism and idealism are equivalent (a supposition advanced, however, on entirely nonempirical grounds).

Realism is, of course, an orientation that emphasizes power and powerholders. Realists tend to emphasize conflict of interest, and scholars under the influence of the realist paradigm tend to believe that change starts at the top and, therefore, that researchers do best to talk to powerholders if they want to get their fingers on the pulse of a society. Realists tend to be conventionalists, that is, to treat laws as the final arbiter in moral questions, and to be impatient with appeals to human reason, conscience, normative standards such as Natural Law, or even, in the case of some realists, normative covenants such as the Universal Declaration of Human Rights. Zvonko Lerotić, a professor of political science at the University of Zagreb and sometime adviser to the late Croatian president Franjo Tudjman, offered a caricature of the realist position in December 1995 in urging (evidently seriously), "Peace is not better than war, nor [is] war better than peace. Justice is not better than injustice, nor [is] injustice better than justice. Neither is virtue better than crime or crime [better] than virtue, unless it leads to realizing the state and national dreams."[6]

Idealism offers a sharply contrasting image of the world. I find myself, indeed, in complete agreement with Chris Brown's assertion that

> ethical considerations have been major sources of change, in particular in Eastern Europe, where the moral bankruptcy of the old order was as apparent as its economic and political failures. . . . Policies guided only by considerations of *Realpolitik* will not succeed in establishing a legitimate order in Europe. New structures will neither merit nor receive public acceptance unless they are seen as ethically defensible.[7]

Idealists tend to emphasize values and norms, and scholars under the influence of the idealist paradigm tend to believe that the most important processes of change tend to start from below, and therefore that researchers endeavoring to keep their fingers on the pulse of society need to talk with people in many walks of life, and to take note of people's notions of what *ought to be* the case in policy. Idealists tend to be universalists, that is, to treat human reason as the final arbiter, and to believe that it is appropriate to judge laws according to standards set by Natural Law or some other external standard, as well as by normative covenants such as the Universal Declaration of Human Rights. Further, where realists take output as the measure of a system's legitimacy (and hence their stress on civil order, prosperity, and the development of strong institutions of state), idealists look rather to the normative structure in assessing a state's (or a system's) legitimacy. It is in this spirit that Thomas Pogge has urged a rethinking of the notion of state sovereignty, proposing that it be deconstructed and dispersed vertically. Characterizing the traditional concept of state sovereignty as "no longer feasible," Pogge argued, instead, that citizens' "allegiance and loyalties should be widely dispersed over these units: neighborhood, town, county, province, state, region, and world at large."[8]

My own version of idealism, grounded in the philosophical writings of John Locke, Immanuel Kant, and James Madison in the first place and having resonance with the thinking of such contemporary writers as Alan Gewirth,[9] Jürgen Habermas,[10] Susan Mendus,[11] John Rawls,[12] Joseph Raz,[13] and Ian Shapiro,[14] starts with the classical liberal notion of Universal Reason, taking that as the starting point for constructing a theory of system legitimacy. It is, thus, on the basis of an appeal to Universal Reason that I take the liberal project (as defined in chapters 1 and 2) as the basis for the moral legitimacy of a given system, and social justice (respecting also the dual principles of equality and sufficiency) as the core of any claim to economic legitimacy. As for political legitimacy, I link this to widespread agreement on certain fixed rules of political succession, with the election of public officials being the principal rule to win such agreement in the contemporary era.[15] That said, it should be obvious in what sense I use the term "liberalism" to refer to a moral understanding, rather than, as Barry Hindess would have it, to "a doctrine of government for the members of the community."[16] Indeed, defining liberalism as a "doctrine of government" blurs the distinction between liberalism and democracy to the extent that one might become unable to imagine illiberal forms of democracy at all.

Do idealists trivialize or disregard power considerations? Of course not. Rather, idealists believe that power does not operate in a normative vacuum, and that the mere endeavor to behave as if there were no universally understood normative standards has operated to bring about the collapse of more than a few authoritarian systems. The repudiation of Natural Law is also a central feature of religious terrorism today.

The chief lesson of 1989, therefore, is that the idealists were and are always right: power without legitimacy cannot last, order without the sanction of legitimate authority is, at most, transitory, ephemeral. Only system legitimacy can provide the foundation for stable political life. The more legitimate a system is (in its moral, political, and economic spheres), the better its chances of stability and endurance. The less legitimate a system (in any of the three specified spheres), the greater the chances that civil order will break down and that the institutions of state will prove unstable. There are all sorts of system equilibria. But only a fully legitimate system can remain at equilibrium for long periods of time; where incumbents corrupt institutions and laws (e.g., by allowing hitherto democratic institutions to evolve into the instruments of plutocratic rule or into weapons for an intolerant religious current), or aggrandize power incompatible with notions of rule of law, they endanger not only their own personal credibility among the population but the system itself. If prolonged, a crisis created by such forms of corruption will condemn the system itself to death.

Hence, to Huntington's dictum that the all-important distinction in politics is between those systems capable of maintaining order and those not so capable, I answer: Do not mistake the smoke for the fire. The fulcrum of politics is always the principle of triadic legitimacy that demarcates differences in system behavior, capacity, stability, and life expectancy. And to the postmodern illusion that there are no moral absolutes and that morality is purely subjective, I answer: The moral law abides in all rational beings, and, while some moral decisions are obscured by uncertainty, others are completely clear. Most people can recognize the difference between honesty and dishonesty, between kindness and cruelty, between generosity and self-serving greed, and it is because of Natural Law, our Universal Reason, that most of us agree on which choice is more virtuous.

NOTES

CHAPTER ONE

1. I retain the traditional term "Eastern Europe" to refer to those European postcommunist states that were not part of the Soviet Union.

2. Sabrina Ramet, *Whose Democracy? Nationalism, Religion, and the Doctrine of Collective Rights in Post-1989 Eastern Europe* (Lanham, Md.: Rowman & Littlefield, 1997).

3. Shashi Tharoor, "Are Human Rights Universal?" *World Policy Journal* 16, no. 4 (1999/2000): 3.

4. See the exposition in Petr Kropotkin, *Mutual Aid: A Factor of Evolution* (Boston: Porter Sargent, 1902), especially the introduction and chaps. 3, 7–8.

5. Heinrich A. Rommen, *The State in Catholic Thought: A Treatise in Political Philosophy* (New York: B. Herder, 1945; reprinted by Greenwood Press, 1969), 155.

6. Here I am evidently following in the footsteps of Polish liberal Mirosław Dzielski, who, in his *Duch nadchodzaego czasu* (Wrocław: Wektory, 1989) reportedly endeavored to identify a common ground between Catholicism and liberalism. See the summary of Dzielski's views in Jerzy Szacki, *Liberalism after Communism* (Budapest: Central European University Press, 1995), 178–80. For further discussions of the relationship between Catholicism and liberalism, see Kenneth L. Grasso, Gerard V. Bradley, and Robert Hunt, eds., *Catholicism, Liberalism, and Communitarianism: The Catholic Intellectual Tradition and the Moral Foundations of Democracy* (Lanham, Md.: Rowman & Littlefield, 1995); John Langan, S. J., "Catholicism and Liberalism—200 Years of Contest and Consensus," in R. Bruce Douglass, Gerald M. Mara, and Henry S. Richardson, eds., *Liberalism and the Good* (New York:

Routledge, 1990); and R. Bruce Douglass and David Hollenbach, eds., *Catholicism and Liberalism: Contributions to American Public Philosophy* (Cambridge: Cambridge University Press, 1994).

7. Aquinas, who did much to develop the theory of Natural Law, also had this to say about civic equality: "Political [as opposed to despotic] government is the leadership of free and equal people; and so the roles of leader and led (ruler and ruled) are swapped about for the sake of equality, and many people get to be constituted ruler either in one position or responsibility or in a number of such positions"; from *In libros Politocorum Aristotelis,* as quoted in John Finnis, "Is Natural Law Theory Compatible with Limited Government?" in Robert George, ed., *Natural Law, Liberalism, and Morality: Contemporary Essays* (Oxford: Clarendon Press, 1996), 2.

8. See Dudley R. Knowles, "A Reformulation of the Harm Principle," *Political Theory* 6, no. 2 (1978): 233–46. Regarding Kant on equality, see Allen W. Wood, *Kant's Ethical Thought* (Cambridge: Cambridge University Press, 1999), 132–39.

9. See Norberto Bobbio, *Thomas Hobbes and the Natural Law Tradition,* trans. by Daniela Gobetti (Chicago: University of Chicago Press, 1993).

10. Thomas Hobbes, Preface to *On the Citizen,* trans. from Latin and ed. by Richard Tuck and Michael Silverthorne (Cambridge: Cambridge University Press, 1998), 9–10.

11. Max Stirner, *The Ego and His Own,* trans. from German by Steven T. Byington, ed. by James J. Martin (New York: Libertarian Book Club, 1963). See also R. W. K. Paterson, *The Nihilist Egoist: Max Stirner* (London: Oxford University Press, 1971).

12. As Stephen Holmes points out rather indirectly in "The Permanent Structure of Antiliberal Thought," in Nancy L. Rosenblum, ed., *Liberalism and the Moral Life* (Cambridge, Mass.: Harvard University Press, 1989), 230.

13. Quoted in Henry S. Richardson, "The Problem of Liberalism and the Good," in Rosenblum, *Liberalism and the Moral Life,* 1.

14. Rommen, *State in Catholic Thought,* 275.

15. Quoted in Rudolf Rocker, *Nationalism and Culture,* trans. from German by Ray E. Chase (Montreal: Black Rose Books, 1998), 174.

CHAPTER TWO

1. L. W. Sumner, *The Moral Foundation of Rights* (New York: Oxford University Press, 1987).

2. John Warren, "The Ethics and Morality of the Ancient Egyptians," at touregypt.net/featurestories.ethics.htm [accessed on 18 July 2006].

3. "Library of Halexandria: Sumerian" (last updated 21 April 2004), at www .halexandria.org/dward183.htm and www.halexandria.org/dward187.htm [accessed on 18 July 2006].

4. Richard Hooker, *Of the Laws of Ecclesiastical Polity,* ed. by Arthur Stephen McGrade (Cambridge: Cambridge University Press, 1989), First Book, 77.

5. John Locke, *Two Treatises of Government,* ed. by Peter Laslett (Cambridge: Cambridge University Press, 1988), Second Treatise, 271 (capitalization as given).

6. See Adrienne Koch, *Jefferson and Madison: The Great Collaboration* (New York: Knopf, 1964); and Gary Rosen, *American Compact: James Madison and the Problem of Founding* (Lawrence, Kan.: University Press of Kansas, 1999).

7. See Thomas Hobbes, *On the citizen,* ed. and trans. from Latin by Richard Tuck and Michael Silverthorne (Cambridge: Cambridge University Press, 1998); and Norberto Bobbio, *Thomas Hobbes and the Natural Law Tradition,* trans. from Italian by Daniela Gobetti (Chicago: University of Chicago Press, 1993).

8. According to Peter Berkowitz, the purpose of the Enlightenment was "to install reason as the one true authority" and therefore "reason is the defining feature of [the] Enlightenment."—Berkowitz, "Enlightenment Rightly Understood," in *Policy Review online,* at www.policyreview.org/dec04/berkowitz.html [accessed on 19 July 2006].

9. See Richard Ashcraft, *Revolutionary Politics and Locke's Two Treatises of Government* (Princeton, N.J.: Princeton University Press, 1986).

10. A particularly extreme example is provided by J. L. Talmon's *The Origin of Totalitarian Democracy* (London: Secker & Warburg, 1952), which argues that the kind of democracy which Rousseau favored was totalitarian in content.

11. Immanuel Kant, *The Metaphysics of Morals,* trans. from German by Mary Gregor (Cambridge: Cambridge University Press, 1991), 51.

12. Immanuel Kant, "Idea for a Universal History with a Cosmopolitan Purpose" (1784), in I. Kant, *Political Writings,* 2nd, enlarged ed., trans. from German by H. B. Nisbet, ed. by Hans Reiss (Cambridge: Cambridge University Press, 1991), 47.

13. Sabrina Ramet, *Thinking about Yugoslavia: Scholarly Debates about the Yugoslav Breakup and the Wars in Bosnia and Kosovo* (Cambridge: Cambridge University Press, 2005), xvii.

14. Kant, *Metaphysics of Morals,* 66.

15. In *Utilitarianism,* Mill refers to Kant as a ". . . remarkable man, whose system of thought will long remain one of the landmarks in the history of philosophical speculation."—John Stuart Mill, *Utilitarianism,* in J. S. Mill, *Utilitarianism, On Liberty, Considerations on Representative Government* (London: Everyman's Library, 1993), 4.

16. Jeremy Bentham, *Anarchical Fallacies: Being an Examination of the Declarations of Rights Issued during the French Revolution* (1823), extracted in Peter Singer (ed.), *Ethics* (Oxford: Oxford University Press, 1994), 271, Bentham's italics.

17. Nicholas Capaldi, "John Stuart Mill's Defense of Liberal Culture," in Eldon J. Eisenach (ed.), *Mill and the Moral Character of Liberalism* (University Park, Pa.: Pennsylvania State University Press, 1998), 85.

18. Quoted in *Ibid.,* 97.

19. Peter Berkowitz, "Liberty, Virtue, and the Discipline of Individuality," in Eisenach (ed.), *Mill and the Moral Character,* 13.

20. Hannah Arendt, *The Origins of Totalitarianism,* new ed. (New York: Harcourt, Brace, & World, 1966).

21. "Justice as Fairness," in *Wikipedia, the free encyclopedia,* at http://en .wikipedia.org/wiki/Justice_as_Fairness [accessed on 22 July 2006].

22. John Rawls, *Political Liberalism* (New York: Columbia University Press, 1993, 1996), 129.

23. Jürgen Habermas, *The Inclusion of the Other: Studies in Political Theory*, ed. by Ciaran Cronin and Pablo De Greif (Cambridge, Mass.: MIT Press, 1998).

24. Christine M. Hassenstab, "'Race Suicide,' Defectives and Vampires: Moral panics and Indiana's sterilization law, 1906–07," manuscript under review.

25. See Christine M. Hassenstab, *The Politics of Reproductive Science: Controversies in the United States and Norway, 1907–2006*, Ph.D. dissertation in progress (for NTNU); and John W. Johnson, *Griswold v. Connecticut: Birth Control and the Constitutional Right of Privacy* (Lawrence, Kansas: University Press of Kansas, 2005).

26. See John C. Green, Mark J. Rozell, and Clyde Wilcox (eds.), *The Christian Right in American Politics: Marching to the Millennium* (Washington D.C.: Georgetown University Press, 2003).

27. Gary L. Francione, *Animals, Property, and the Law* (Philadelphia: Temple University Press, 1995), 67.

28. See David DeGrazia, "On the Question of Personhood beyond *Homo sapiens*," in Peter Singer (ed.), *In Defense of Animals: The Second Wave* (Oxford: Blackwell, 2006), 40–53.

CHAPTER THREE

1. Laura D'Andrea Tyson, "The Three Challenges of Economic Transition in Eastern Europe," in George W. Breslauer, ed., *Dilemmas of Transition in the Soviet Union and Eastern Europe* (Berkeley: Center for Slavic and East European Studies, 1991), 45, 47–49, 63.

2. Ivo Banac, "Introduction," in Ivo Banac, ed., *Eastern Europe in Revolution* (Ithaca, N.Y.: Cornell University Press, 1992), 11; Katherine Verdery and Gail Kligman, "Romania after Ceauşescu: Post-Communist Communism?" in ibid., 140; Elez Biberaj, "Albania: The Last Domino," in ibid., 205.

3. András Kepes, "The Current Political Background of the Economic Transition in Hungary," in Breslauer, *Dilemmas of Transition*, 125.

4. Ken Jowitt, "The Leninist Legacy," in Banac, *Eastern Europe in Revolution*, 222–23.

5. Patricia J. Smith, "German Economic and Monetary Union: Transition to a Market Economy," in Sabrina Petra Ramet, ed., *Adaptation and Transformation in Communist and Post-Communist Systems* (Boulder, Colo.: Westview Press, 1992), 42.

6. Anneli Uti Gabanyi, *Die unvollendete Revolution. Rumänien seit 1945* (Munich: Piper Verlag, 1990). See also Gabanyi, *Systemwechsel in Rumänien. Von der Revolution zur Transformaton* (Munich: R. Oldenbourg Verlag, 1998).

7. Enikő Bollobás, "Hungary: Post-Communist Trends and Prospects" (November 1991), in Constantine Menges, ed., *Transitions from Communism in Russia and Eastern Europe: Analysis and Perspectives* (Lanham, Md.: University Press of America, 1994), 106.

8. György Tokay and Dorin Tudoran, "Romania: Is There a Transition to Democracy?" (April 1992), in Menges, *Transitions from Communism*, 136.

9. Sabrina Petra Ramet, "Processes of Decay, Engines of Transformation: An Introduction," in Ramet, *Adaptation and Transformation*, 7, 8. The book was finalized in 1991.

10. Sabrina Petra Ramet, "The New Poland: Democratic and Authoritarian Tendencies," *Global Affairs* 7, no. 2 (1992): 135.

11. Ivo Banac, "Yugoslavia: The Road to Civil War," paper presented at the annual convention of the American Association for the Advancement of Slavic Studies, Washington, D.C., November 1990, 3, as cited in Reneo Lukić and Allen Lynch, *Europe from the Balkans to the Urals: The Disintegration of Yugoslavia and the Soviet Union* (Oxford: Oxford University Press, 1996), 156.

12. Meier later drew upon his interviews and research to produce a highly successful volume concentrating, above all, on the years 1980–91; see Viktor Meier, *Yugoslavia: A History of Its Demise,* trans. from German by Sabrina Ramet (London: Routledge, 1999).

13. Kazimierz Z. Poznański, "Property Rights Perspective on Evolution of Communist-Type Economies," in Kazimierz Z. Poznański, ed., *Constructing Capitalism: The Reemergence of Civil Society and Liberal Economy in the Post-Communist World* (Boulder, Colo.: Westview Press, 1992), 78.

14. Kazimierz Z. Poznański, "Post-Communist Transition as Institutional Disintegration: Explaining the Regional Economic Recession," *Acta Oeconomica* 50, nos. 1–2 (1999): 6.

15. Sabrina Petra Ramet, *Social Currents in Eastern Europe: The Sources and Consequences of the Great Transformation,* 2d ed. (Durham, N.C.: Duke University Press, 1995), 374.

16. *Financial Times,* 2 December 1991, 2, at www.lexisnexis.com/academic/universe/.

17. Agence France Presse (Paris), 16 December 1991, at www.lexisnexis.com/academic/universe/.

18. See the table in Sabrina Ramet, *Whose Democracy? Nationalism, Religion, and the Doctrine of Collective Rights in Post-1989 Eastern Europe* (Lanham, Md.: Rowman & Littlefield, 1997), 40.

19. On Serbs, 1 Net Web site (Belgrade), 10 January 2000, in BBC Summary of World Broadcasts, 13 January 2000; on Romanians, *Interfax news agency,* 22 October 1999, in *BBC Monitoring Europe–Political,* 22 October 1999; on Albanians, *M2 Presswire,* 5 May 1999; on Bulgarians, BTA (Sofia), 15 February 1999, in *BBC Monitoring Europe–Economic,* 15 February 1999—all at www.lexisnexis.com/academic/universe/.

20. Conversation with Kazimierz Z. Poznański, Lynnwood, Washington, 12 February 2000. Poznański deals with the failure of transition in Poland in extenso in his book *Wielki przekręt: Klęska polskich reform* (Warsaw: Towarzystwo Wydawnicze i Literackie, 2000).

21. Kazimierz Z. Poznański, "The Morals of Transition: Decline of Public Interest and Runaway Reforms in Eastern Europe," in Sorin Antohi and Vladimir Tismaneanu, eds., *Between Past and Future: The Revolutions of 1989 and Their Aftermath* (Budapest: Central European University Press, 2000), 235.

22. Conversation with Kazimierz Z. Poznański, Seattle, Washington, 18 February 2000.

23. Branka Nanevska, "The Sale of [the] Macedonian Economy," *AIM Press*, 3 February 2000, 2, at www.aimpress.org.

24. *Financial News* (London), 15 May 2000, 31 July 2000, 14 September 2003, 28 March 2004, 15 September 2003, and 3 September 2003—all at www.newsbank.com/govlib/awn.

25. Kosovo, *Kosova Report*, 27 October 2005; and Republika Srpska, *SeeNews*, 23 January 2006, at www.lexisnexis.com/academic/universe/.

26. *International Herald Tribune,* 4 June 1997, at www.iht.com (accessed 8 November 2005).

27. Bulgarian National Radio, 6 January 2006, at www.bnr.bg/ (accessed 25 January 2006).

28. Reuters, 24 Occtober 2005, at today.reuters.com/ (accessed 8 November 2005).

29. *Times* (London), 1 May 2005, at www.timesonline.co.uk/ (accessed 2 May 2005).

30. *Economist* (London), 25 June 2005, "Meet the neighbours" supplement, 6.

31. Derek Monroe, "Poland: 25 Years after Solidarity," *Ohmy News,* February 2005, at english.ohmynews.com/ (accessed 19 March 2006).

32. Sabrina Ramet, "The Failure of Transition in the Balkans: An Introduction," in *Modern Greek Studies Yearbook,* vol. 16/17 (Minneapolis: Modern Greek Studies Program, 2000–2001), 279.

33. C. B. MacPherson, *The Political Theory of Possessive Individualism: Hobbes to Locke* (Oxford: Oxford University Press, 1962), 199.

34. John Locke, *Two Treatises of Government,* ed. by Peter Laslett (Cambridge: Cambridge University Press, 1960), 2:291, my emphasis.

35. On this point, see also W. M. Spellman, *John Locke* (New York: St. Martin's Press, 1997), 115–16.

36. L. T. Hobhouse, *Liberalism* (London: Oxford University Press, 1911; reprinted, 1981), 67, 70, my emphasis.

37. Ibid., 97, 101–102, 105, 107–108.

38. In Ramet, *Whose Democracy,* introduction, cha 3, conclusion.

39. Or, for that matter, see Robert Grant, "Liberalism, Values, and Social Cohesion," in Zdeněk Suda and Jiří Musil, eds., *The Meaning of Liberalism: East and West* (Budapest: Central European University Press, 2000), 74.

40. John Paul II, *Encyclical Letter "Centisumus Annus" of the Supreme Pontiff* (Boston: St. Paul Books, 1991), 25–26.

41. L. W. Sumner, *The Moral Foundation of Rights* (Oxford: Clarendon Press,

1987); Russell Hardin, *Morality within the Limits of Reason* (Chicago: University of Chicago Press, 1988).

42. Jerzy Szacki notes the general unconsciousness about political liberalism in postcommunist Poland; see his excellent and insightful *Liberalism after Communism* (Budapest: Central European University Press, 1995), 202–203.

43. John Paul II, *Centisimus Annus,* 16.

44. Szacki, *Liberalism after Communism,* 199.

45. Zdenęk Suda, "Liberalism in Central Europe after 1989," in Suda and Musil, *Meaning of Liberalism,* 200.

CHAPTER FOUR

1. See, for example, Yael Tamir, *Liberal Nationalism* (Princeton, N.J.: Princeton University Press, 1993).

2. Jamie Mayerfeld, "The Myth of Benign Group Identity: A Critique of Liberal Nationalism," *Polity* 30, no. 4 (1998): 557–58.

3. Norberto Bobbio, *Thomas Hobbes and the Natural Law Tradition,* trans. from Italian by Daniela Gobetti (Chicago: University of Chicago Press, 1993).

4. James R. Hurtgen, "Hobbes's Theory of Sovereignty in *Leviathan,*" *Reason Papers* 5 (1979): 64–65.

5. Leo Strauss, *The Political Philosophy of Hobbes: Its Basis and Its Genesis,* trans. from German by Elsa M. Sinclair (Chicago: University of Chicago Press, 1963), 66.

6. Ibid., 66–67.

7. Thomas Hobbes, *A Dialogue between a Philosopher and a Student of the Common Laws of England,* ed. by Joseph Cropsey (Chicago: University of Chicago Press, 1971), 69, 71.

8. See Thomas Hobbes, *Leviathan,* ed. Michael Oakeshott (Toronto: Collier Books, 1971).

9. Edmund Morgan, *Inventing the People: The Rise of Popular Sovereignty in England and America* (New York: W. W. Norton, 1988), 58–60.

10. Thomas Hobbes, *On the Citizen,* ed. and trans. by Richard Tuck and Michael Silverthorne (Cambridge: Cambridge University Press, 1988), 76.

11. Charles E. Merriam Jr., *History of the Theory of Sovereignty since Rousseau* (New York: Garland, 1972; reprint of the 1900 edition), 25.

12. Arnold A. Rogow, *Thomas Hobbes: Radical in the Service of Reaction* (New York: W. W. Norton, 1986), 139. See also Hobbes, *On the Citizen,* 135.

13. Hobbes, *On the Citizen,* 80.

14. Ibid., 147, 152.

15. Ibid., 245. Regarding, Hobbes's views on absolute sovereignty, see also A. Martinich, *Hobbes: A Biography* (Cambridge: Cambridge University Press, 1999), 151–53.

16. Rogow, *Thomas Hobbes,* 245.

17. Quoted in Carol Blum, *Rousseau and the Republic of Virtue: The Lan-*

guage of Politics in the French Revolution (Ithaca, N.Y.: Cornell University Press, 1986), 161.

18. The portrayal of Rousseau as a democrat is, on the other hand, disputed by W. J. Stankiewicz; see Stankiewicz's introduction, "In Defense of Sovereignty: A Critique and an Interpretation," in W. J. Stankiewicz, ed., *In Defense of Sovereignty* (New York: Oxford University Press, 1969), 27. See also Jacques Maritain, "The Concept of Sovereignty," in ibid., 57–58.

19. David Rosenfeld, "Rousseau's Unanimous Contract and the Doctrine of Popular Sovereignty," *History of Political Thought* 8, no. 1 (1987): 83, 84.

20. Ibid., 87, 89.

21. J. W. Chapman, *Rousseau—Totalitarian or Liberal?* (1956), 139, as quoted in J. McManners, "The Social Contract and Rousseau's Revolt against Society," in Maurice Cranston and Richard S. Peters, eds., *Hobbes and Rousseau: A Collection of Critical Essays* (Garden City, N.Y.: Anchor Books, 1972), 294.

22. Ali A. Mazrui, "Alienable Sovereignty in Rousseau: A Further Look," *Ethics* 77, no. 2 (1967): 107.

23. J. L. Talmon, *The Origins of Totalitarian Democracy* (London: Secker & Warburg, 1952).

24. Jean-Jacques Rousseau, "The Social Contract," in *Social Contract*, ed. Sir Ernest Barker (Oxford: Oxford University Press, 1960), 193.

25. Ibid., 180.

26. Ibid., 175.

27. See Blum, *Rousseau and the Republic of Virtue*, 242. For further discussion of the problematic relationship between liberalism and democracy, see John Kekes, *Against Liberalism* (Ithaca, N.Y.: Cornell University Press, 1997), esp. chaps. 1 and 8.

28. These criticisms are mentioned in Ian Shapiro, *The Moral Foundations of Politics* (New Haven, Conn.: Yale University Press, 2003), 190–95.

29. Ibid., p 200–23.

30. For example, see Wojciech Sokolewicz, "The Relevance of Western Models for Constitution-Building in Poland," in Joachim Jens Hesse and Nevil Johnson, eds., *Constitutional Policy and Change in Europe* (Oxford: Oxford University Press, 1995), 252–53.

31. Rousseau, "Social Contract," 231.

32. Immanuel Kant, "Perpetual Peace," as quoted in Matthew Levinger, "Kant and the Origins of Prussian Constitutionalism," *History of Political Thought* 19, no. 2 (1998): 245.

33. Immanuel Kant, "The Contest of the Faculties," as quoted in Levinger, "Kant and the Origins," 244.

34. Immanuel Kant, "Perpetual Peace," in *Political Writings*, ed. by Hans Reiss (Cambridge: Cambridge University Press, 1970), 101.

35. On this point, see Sven Arntzen, "Kant's Denial of Absolute Sovereignty," *Pacific Philosophical Quarterly* 76, no. 1 (1995): 1–3; and Levinger, "Kant and the Origins," 244.

36. Allen W. Wood, *Kant's Ethical Thought* (Cambridge: Cambridge University Press, 1999), 248.

37. See Ramet, *Whose Democracy? Nationalism, Religion, and the Doctrine of Collective Rights in Post-1989 Eastern Europe* (Lanham, Md.: Rowman & Littlefield, 1997), introduction.

38. Immanuel Kant, *The Metaphysics of Morals,* trans. from German by Mary Gregor (Cambridge: Cambridge University Press, 1991), 130, 131.

39. See Peter Nicholson, "Kant on the Duty Never to Resist the Sovereign," *Ethics* 86, no. 3 (1976): 218–19; and Arntzen, "Kant's Denial," 4–5. See also comments in Heiner Bielefeldt, "Autonomy and Republicanism: Immanuel Kant's Philosophy of Freedom," *Political Theory* 25, no. 4 (1997): 535, 551.

40. Hobbes, *On the Citizen,* 78–79; and Hobbes, *Leviathan,* 129, 132.

41. Immanuel Kant, "On the Common Saying: This May Be True in Theory, but It Does Not Apply in Practice," in *Political Writings,* 74.

42. Wood, *Kant's Ethical Thought,* 229.

43. Donald V. Kommers and W. J. Thompson, "Fundamentals in the Liberal Constitutional Tradition," in Hesse and Johnson, *Constitutional Policy,* 35–36.

44. This argument has been effectively advanced in Jack Snyder, *From Voting to Violence: Democratization and Nationalist Conflict* (New York: W. W. Norton, 2000).

45. These and other extracts from constitutional charters are taken from *The Rebirth of Democracy: 12 Constitutions of Central and Eastern Europe,* 2d ed. (Strasbourg: Council of Europe, 1996).

46. Quoted in Georg Brunner, *Nationality Problems and Minority Conflicts in Eastern Europe* (Gütersloh: Bertelsmann Foundation, 1996), 47.

47. *Nacional* (Zagreb), no. 224 (2 March 2000), at www.nacional.hr/htm/224053.EN.htm.

48. See Julie Mostov, "Democracy and the Politics of National Identity," *Studies in East European Thought* 46, nos. 1–2 (1994): 17–18.

49. John Locke, *Two Treatises of Government,* ed. Peter Laslett (New York: Mentor Books, 1963), 1:247, my emphasis.

50. Ibid., 2:316, 318.

51. Quoted in *Washington Post,* 26 May 1997, A24.

52. Quoted in *Tages-Anzeiger,* 12 May 1997, 3.

53. John I. Ishiyama and Marijke Breuning, *Ethnopolitics in the New Europe* (Boulder: Lynne Rienner, 1998), 7.

54. See Trond Gilberg, *Nationalism and Communism in Romania: The Rise and Fall of Ceaușescu's Personal Dictatorship* (Boulder, Colo.: Westview Press, 1990), 175–76, 179.

55. See Dirk Philipsen, *We Were the People: Voices from East Germany's Revolutionary Autumn of 1989* (Durham, N.C.: Duke University Press, 1993).

56. Liah Greenfeld, *Nationalism: Five Roads to Modernity* (Cambridge, Mass.: Harvard University Press, 1992).

57. Tamir, *Liberal Nationalism* (see note 1, above).

58. Vladimir Tismaneanu, "Nationalism, Populism, and Other Threats to Liberal Democracy in Post-Communist Europe," *Donald W. Treadgold Papers in Russian, East European, and Central Asian Studies,* no. 20 (Seattle: Henry M. Jackson School of International Studies of the University of Washington, January 1999).

59. Bernard Yack, "Reconciling Liberalism and Democracy," *Political Theory* 23, no. 1 (1995): 166–82; and Yack, "Popular Sovereignty and Nationalism," *Political Theory* 29, no. 4 (2001): 517–36.

60. Iris Young, *Justice and the Politics of Difference* (Princeton, N.J.: Princeton University Press, 1990).

61. Andrew Mason, "Political Community, Liberal-Nationalism, and the Ethics of Assimilation," *Ethics* 109, no. 2 (1999): 261–86.

62. See Omar Dahbour, review article in *Constellations* 3, no. 1 (1996): 129–32.

63. Ramet, *Whose Democracy* (see note 37, above).

64. Mason, "Political Community, Liberal-Nationalism," 271–72.

65. As quoted in Tismaneanu, "Nationalism, Populism," 41–42.

CHAPTER FIVE

1. Robert Redslob, *Le Principe des Nationalités* (1931), as quoted in Nathaniel Berman, "'But the Alternative Is Despair': Nationalism and the Modernist Renewal of International Law," *Harvard Law Review* 106, no. 8 (1993): 1810.

2. On group rights, see Russell Hardin, *Morality within the Limits of Reason* (Chicago: University of Chicago Press, 1988), 96–97.

3. Reneo Lukić and Allen Lynch, *Europe from the Balkans to the Urals: The Disintegration of Yugoslavia and the Soviet Union* (Oxford: Oxford University Press, 1996), 33.

4. Immanuel Kant, *The Metaphysics of Morals,* trans. from German by Mary Gregor (Cambridge: Cambridge University Press, 1991); and Sabrina Ramet, *Whose Democracy? Nationalism, Religion, and the Doctrine of Collective Rights in Post-1989 Eastern Europe* (Lanham, Md.: Rowman & Littlefield, 1997).

5. David Calleo, "Reflections on the Idea of the Nation-State," in Charles A. Kupchan, ed., *Nationalism and Nationalities in the New Europe* (Ithaca, N.Y.: Cornell University Press, 1995), 23.

6. Ibid.

7. Hans J. Morgenthau, *Politics among Nations: The Struggle for Power and Peace,* 5th ed. (New York: Alfred A. Knopf, 1973), 6–9.

8. See G. W. F. Hegel, *Reason in History: A General Introduction to the Philosophy of History,* trans. from German by Robert S. Hartman (Indianapolis: Bobbs-Merrill, 1953).

9. Morgenthau, *Politics among Nations,* 5. See also Niccolo Machiavelli, *The Prince and the Discourses,* trans. from Italian by Luigi Ricci, rev. by E. R. Vincent (New York: Modern Library, 1950).

10. *Washington Post,* 6 June 1998, A18.

11. Thomas Hobbes, *On the Citizen,* ed. and trans. by Richard Tuck and Michael Silverthorne (Cambridge: Cambridge University Press, 1998), 132.

12. For example, by Charles W. Kegley, Jr., and Eugene R. Wittkopf, in their *World Politics: Trend and Transformation,* 2d ed. (New York: St. Martin's Press, 1985), 17.

13. Karl Jaspers, *Kant,* trans. from German by Ralph Manheim (San Diego: Harcourt Brace, 1962), 116, 118; and Kurt Taylor Gaubatz, "Kant, Democracy, and History," *Journal of Democracy* 7, no. 4 (1996): 138, 147–48.

14. Kant, *Metaphysics of Morals,* 156. See also Hannah Arendt, *Lectures on Kant's Political Philosophy* (Chicago: University of Chicago Press, 1982), 52–54; and Michael W. Doyle, "Liberalism and International Relations," in Ronald Beiner and William James Booth, eds., *Kant & Political Philosophy: The Contemporary Legacy* (New Haven, Conn.: Yale University Press, 1993), 186–93.

15. Jaspers, *Kant,* 114.

16. Jacob Rogozinski, "It Makes Us Wrong: Kant and Radical Evil," in Joan Copjec, ed., *Radical Evil* (London: Verso, 1996), 31–32.

17. Morgenthau, *Politics among Nations,* 10.

18. See Götz Aly, Peter Chroust, and Christian Pross, *Cleansing the Fatherland: Nazi Medicine and Racial Hygiene,* trans. from German by Belinda Cooper (Baltimore, Md.: Johns Hopkins University Press, 1994); and George J. Annas and Michael A. Grodin, eds., *The Nazi Doctors and the Nuremberg Code: Human Rights in Human Experimentation* (New York: Oxford University Press, 1992).

19. Carol S. Lilly, "Amoral Realism or Immoral Obfuscation?" *Slavic Review* 55, no. 4 (1996): 749.

20. Edward Hallett Carr, *The Twenty Years' Crisis, 1919–1939: An Introduction to the Study of International Relations* (New York: Harper & Row, 1964), 8.

21. Bernard Williams, a foe of relativism, summarizing its principal propositions in his *Morality: An Introduction to Ethics* (New York: Harper & Row, 1972), 20, as quoted in Ruth Macklin, "Universality of the Nuremberg Code," in Annas and Grodin, *Nazi Doctors,* 241.

22. Lilly, "Amoral Realism," 752.

23. Joseph Raz, "Autonomy, Toleration, and the Harm Principle," in Susan Mendus, ed., *Justifying Toleration: Conceptual and Historical Perspectives* (Cambridge: Cambridge University Press, 1988), 157, 165.

24. See John Spanier, *American Foreign Policy since World War II,* 6th ed. (New York: Praeger, 1973).

25. Alan Gewirth, *The Community of Rights* (Chicago: University of Chicago Press, 1996), 41.

26. A. J. Taylor, *From Sarajevo to Potsdam* (London: Thames & Hudson, 1965).

27. Kant, *Metaphysics of Morals,* 133.

28. Regarding natural rights and positive rights, see J. W. Harris, *Legal Philosophies,* 2d ed. (London: Butterworths, 1997).

29. If even one state did not permit such secession, then the right could not be said to be a universal positive right.

30. John Keane, *Reflections on Violence* (London: Verso, 1996).

31. For a discussion of these moral theories, see L. W. Sumner, *The Moral Foundation of Rights* (Oxford: Clarendon Press, 1987).

32. Kant, *Metaphysics of Morals,* 56.

33. John Stuart Mill, *On Liberty and Other Writings* (Cambridge: Cambridge University Press, 1989), 8.

34. Immanuel Kant, *The Moral Law: Groundwork of the Metaphysic of Morals,* trans. from German by H. J. Paton (London: Routledge, 1995 [reprint of 1948 ed.]), 67, emphasis omitted.

35. Kant, *Metaphysics of Morals,* 51.

36. Rein Mullerson, "New Developments in the Former USSR and Yugoslavia," *Virginia Journal of International Law* 33, no. 2 (1993), es 313.

37. Conventionalism's limitations are summarized in Sumner, *Moral Foundation.*

38. Mary Gregor, "Kant on 'Natural Rights,'" in Beiner and Booth, *Kant & Political Philosophy,* 52.

39. Quoted in ibid., 66.

40. Chandran Kukathas, "Are There Any Cultural Rights?" and Will Kymlicka, "The Rights of Minority Cultures: Reply to Kukathas"—both in *Political Theory* 20, no. 1 (1992); and Chandran Kukathas, "Cultural Rights Again: A Rejoinder to Kymlicka," *Political Theory* 20, no. 4 (1992). See also Will Kymlicka, ed., *The Rights of Minority Cultures* (Oxford: Oxford University Press, 1995).

41. Ramet, *Whose Democracy?* cha 3 and conclusion.

42. Quoted in Lloyd L. Weinreb, "The Moral Point of View," in Robert George, ed., *Natural Law, Liberalism, and Morality* (Oxford: Clarendon Press, 1996), 200–201.

43. See Norberto Bobbio, *Thomas Hobbes and the Natural Law Tradition,* trans. from Italian by Daniela Gobetti (Chicago: University of Chicago Press, 1993).

44. Kant, *Moral Law: Groundwork,* 104. See also Kant, *Metaphysics of Morals,* 53; and Jaspers, *Kant,* 68. The implications of Kant's metaphysics for organized religion were well understood. In fact, to take one example, *American Catholic Quarterly Review* published at least seven critical rebuttals of Kant's thought between 1911 and 1923. In 1911, Simon Fitzsimons charged that "Kant's treatment of the proofs for the existence of a Supreme Being . . . is in the highest degree disingenuous" and accused the German philosopher of sophistry. In 1922, Joseph Schabert contributed an article to the same journal, arguing that "Kant's . . . philosophy is like a watershed whence the stream of speculation flows down to modern idealism, agnosticism, and even materialism." Again, in 1923, yet another writer, Simon Flimons, suggested that "the two forces which, in modern times, have done most to confuse men's minds on the vital question of religion, are agnosticism and the theory of evolution. Of the former, Kant is the progenitor—indeed the protagonist." Fitzsimons, "Criticisms in

Kant: Kant and the Existence of God," *American Catholic Quarterly Review* 36 (April 1911): 313; Schabert, "Kant's Influence on His Successors," *American Catholic Quarterly Review* 47 (January 1922): 120; and Flimons, "Kant and the Proofs for the Existence of God," *American Catholic Quarterly Review* 48 (January 1923): 14.

45. Kant, *Moral Law: Groundwork,* 75.

46. For further discussion of these ideas, see Ramet, *Whose Democracy?* introduction, es 6–13.

47. Ibid., 7.

48. As Kant writes, "To interfere with the use of a piece of land by the first occupant is to wrong him. Natural Right lays down taking first possession as a rightful basis for acquisition on which every first possessor can rely"; *Metaphysics of Morals,* 73.

49. This position was, however, seriously argued by Hans-Hermann Hoppe in his "The Western State as Paradigm," *Society* 35, no. 5 (1998). For my rebuttal of his argument, see Sabrina Ramet, "Profit Motives in Secession," *Society* 35, no. 5 (1998).

50. Fritz Kern, *Kingship and Law in the Middle Ages* (Oxford: Basil Blackwell, 1939).

51. Such as David Miller, *On Nationality* (Oxford: Clarendon Press, 1995), cha 4; and Ernest Gellner, *Nations and Nationalisms* (Oxford: Basil Blackwell, 1983), 2. But for a sophisticated defense of a "soft" and, by his own admission, "vague" right of national self-determination, see Allen Buchanan, "The Morality of Secession," in Kymlicka, *Rights of Minority Cultures,* 350–74.

52. For an extended argument as to why both hegemonist and autonomist/separatist forms of nationalism are dangerous, see Ramet, *Whose Democracy?* chaps. 3, 5–6.

CHAPTER SIX

1. See Joseph Raz, "Autonomy, Toleration, and the Harm Principle," in Susan Mendus (ed.), *Justifying Toleration: Conceptual and Historical Perspectives* (Cambridge: Cambridge University Press, 1988), es 157, 165.

2. Joseph Cardinal Ratzinger [the present Pope Benedict XVI], in interview with Vittorio Messori, *The Ratzinger Report,* trans. from German by Salvator Attanasio and Graham Harrison (San Francisco: St. Ignatius Press, 1985), 51–61.

3. *The HarperCollins Encyclopedia of Catholicism,* Richard McBrien general editor (San Francisco: Harper, 1995), 767.

4. PAP News Wire (1 May 1995), at www.lexisnexis.com/academic/universe/.

5. PAP News Wire (9 March 1997), in *NewsBank*—www.newsbank.com/govlib/awn.

6. Adam Hetnal, "The Polish Catholic Church in Pre- and Post-1989 Poland: An Evaluation," in *East European Quarterly,* Vol. 32, No. 4 (Winter 1988), 515.

7. Both quotes from Sabrina Ramet, *Whose Democracy: Nationalism, Religion, and the Doctrine of Collective Rights in Post-1989 Eastern Europe* (Lanham, Md.: Rowman & Littlefield, 1997), 106.

8. PAP News Agency (28 September 2000), in *NewsBank*—www.newsbank .com/govlib/awn.

9. For further discussion, see Sabrina Ramet, "Thy Will be Done: The Catholic Church and Politics in Poland since 1989," in Timothy A. Byrnes and Peter J. Katzenstein (eds.), *Religion in an Expanding Europe* (Cambridge: Cambridge University Press, 2006).

10. *Gazeta Wyborcza* (10 March 2005), 1, trans. in *Polish News Bulletin* (17 March 2005), via www.lexisnexis.com/academic/universe/; and *Gazeta Wyborcza* (29 April 2005), trans. in *BBC Monitoring Europe—Political* (29 April 2005), via www.lexisnexis.com/academic/universe/.

11. PAP News Wire (8 March 2005), in www.lexisnexis.com/academic/universe/. For background concerning Radio Maryja's problematic relations with the Polish hierarchy, see Ramet, "Thy Will be Done."

12. *Polityka* (Warsaw), 10 September 2005, 18–19, trans. in *Polish News Bulletin* (15 September 2005), via www.lexisnexis.com/academic/universe/.

13. Quoted in *The Irish Times* (22 September 2005), 10, at www.lexisnexis.com/academic/universe/.

14. Quoted in Agence France Presse (25 September 2005), at www .lexisnexis.com/academic/universe/ (one preposition was changed for reasons of syntax).

15. *International Herald Tribune* (24 October 2005), 1, at www.lexisnexis.com/academic/universe/; and *International Herald Tribune* (25 October 2005), 5, at www .lexisnexis.com/academic/universe/.

16. Quoted in *The Independent* (London), 24 December 2005, at www .lexisnexis.com/academic/universe/.

17. Quoted in *International Herald Tribune* (24 October 2005), 1, at www .lexisnexis.com/academic/universe/.

18. Quoted in *The Irish Times* (24 December 2005), 12, at www.lexisnexis.com/academic/universe/.

19. *Polish News Bulletin* (21 December 2005), at www.newsbank.com/govlib/awn.

20. PAP News Wire (4 November 2005), at www.lexisnexis.com/academic/universe/.

21. PAP (6 November 2005), in *BBC Worldwide Monitoring* (6 November 2005), via www.lexisnexis.com/academic/universe/.

22. PAP (22 December 2005), in *BBC Monitoring Europe—Political* (22 December 2005), via www.lexisnexis.com/academic/universe/; and Agence France Presse (10 January 2006), in www.lexisnexis.com/academic/universe/.

23. See Agence France Presse (2 February 2006), at www.lexisnexis.com/academic/universe/.

24. Agence France Presse (3 December 2004), at www.lexisnexis.com/academic/universe/.

25. Robert Biedron, President of the Campaign Against Homophobia, in interview with the author, Warsaw, 24 June 2004.

26. Agence France Presse (20 November 2004), at www.lexisnexis.com/academic/universe/.

27. Agence France Presse (6 March 2005), at www.lexisnexis.com/academic/universe/.

28. Senator Maria Szyszkowska, in interview with the author (Ania Konieczna, interpreter), Warsaw, 6 July 2004.

29. Agence France Presse (3 December 2004), at www.lexisnexis.com/academic/universe/.

30. Quoted in Agence France Presse (8 March 2005), at www.lexisnexis.com/academic/universe/.

31. PAP News Wire (9 May 2005), atwww.lexisnexis.com/academic/universe/.

32. Agence France Presse (18 June 2005), at www.lexisnexis.com/academic/universe/.

33. Krzysztof Kosela,, Tadeusz Szawiel, Miroslawa Grabowska, and Malgorzata Sikorska, *Tozsamosc Polakow a Unia Europejska* (Warszawa: Instytut Badan nad Podstawami Demokracji, 2002), 21.

34. *The Irish Times* (13 June 2005), 9, at www.lexisnexis.com/academic/universe/; and Deutsche Presse-Agentur (19 November 2005), at www.lexisnexis.com/academic/universe/.

35. Agence France Presse (19 November 2005), at www.lexisnexis.com/academic/universe/.

36. When I talked with Senator Szyszkowska in July 2004 (note 28), she told me that she too had never heard of any bishop condemning attacks on gays and lesbians—not even the use of acid.

37. *The Irish Times* (13 June 2005), 9, at www.lexisnexis.com/academic/universe/.

38. PAP News Wire (9 August 2005), at www.lexisnexis.com/academic/universe/.

39. Lisa Keen, "Gays face hostilities in Eastern Europe," in *Bay Area Reporter* (2 March 2006), at www.ebar.com/common/inc/article_print.php?sec=news&article=608, 2.

40. Quoted in *Ibid.*, 2.

41. Quoted in Agence France Presse (31 January 2006), at www.lexisnexis.com/academic/universe/.

42. Quoted in *Gazeta Wyborcza* (1 February 2006), 5, in *Polish News Bulletin* (1 February 2006), via www.lexisnexis.com/academic/universe/.

43. Krzysztof Kosela, "Religijnosc mlodych Niemcow i Polakow," in *Socjologia Religii* (Poznan), Vol. 2 (2004), 125.

44. Krzysztof Kosela, *Splatana tozsamosc* (Warszawa: Wydawnictwo IFiS PAN, 2003), 60.

45. Wanda Nowicka, President of the Federation for Woman and Family Planning, in interview with the author, Warsaw, 22 June 2004.

46. Deutsche Presse-Agentur (25 April 2005), at www.lexisnexis.com/academic/universe/.

47. *Polish News Bulletin* (8 February 2006), at www.newsbank.com/govlib/awn.

48. The other three countries criticized were Belgium, France, and Germany. See *Polish News Bulletin* (15 June 2006), at www.newsbank.com/govlib/awn.

49. PAP News Agency (21 June 2006), at www.newsbank.com/govlib/awn.

50. Quoted in *BBC News* (6 July 2006), at newsvote.bbc.co.uk/.

51. See A. Ambrüz, "Nemít, a tudíž nebit," in *Listy* (Praha), Vol. 45, no. 8 (1995), 40.

52. CTK, 7 November 1995 and 22 February 1996, both on *Nexis*.

53. Joan O'Mahony, "The Catholic Church and Civil Society: Democratic Options in the Post-Communist Czech Republic," in *West European Politics,* Vol. 26, No. 1 (2003), 184.

54. *Prague Post* (21 August 1996), at www.praguepost.com [accessed on 21 October 2004].

55. Jonathan Luxmoore, "Ten Years After the Velvet Revolution, Czech Monasteries Struggle to Survive," in *Christianity Today* (posted 5/10/2000), at www.christianitytoday.com [accessed on 29 December 2004].

56. *Frankfurter Allgemeine* (10 January 1994), 10.

57. CTK (1 February 1996), on *Nexis*.

58. O'Mahony, "The Catholic Church and Civil Society," 182–83.

59. Jonathan Luxmoore, "Eastern Europe 1997–2000: a Review of Church Life," in *Religion, State & Society,* Vol. 29, No. 4 (December 2001), 320–21.

60. *Prague Post* (22 July 1998), at www.praguepost.com [accessed on 21 October 2004]; and *National Catholic Reporter* (19 February 1999), at natcath.org/ORG_Online/archives [accessed on 29 December 2004].

61. *Prague Post* (13 January 1999), at www.praguepost.com [accessed on 21 October 2004]; and *Prague Post* (10 July 2003), at www.praguepost.com [accessed on 21 October 2004].

62. CTK News Agency (Prague), 1 August 2005, at www.newsbank.com/govlib/awn [infoweb.newsbank.com].

63. CTK News Agency (24 October 2005), at www.lexisnexis.com/academic/universe/.

64. According to Pavel Dostal, Minister of Culture, as cited in CTK (14 March 2002), at www.lexisnexis.com/academic/universe/.

65. *Prague Post* (10 February 2005), at www.praguepost.com [accessed on 20 November 2005]. See also *Deutsche Presse-Agentur* (7 February 2005), at www.newsbank.com/govlib/awn.

66. CTK News Agency (21 May 2003), in *BBC Monitoring International Reports* (21 May 2003), via www.lexisnexis.com/academic/universe/; and CTK News Agency (16 December 2003), at www.lexisnexis.com/academic/universe/.

67. CTK News Agency (23 July 2002) and CTK News Agency (25 July 2002)—both at www.lexisnexis.com/academic/universe/.

68. CTK News Agency (21 February 2006), at www.newsbank.com/govlib/awn.

69. U.S. Department of State, *International Religious Freedom Report 2004—Czech Republic* (Washington D.C., released 15 September 2004), at www.state.gov/g/drl/rls/irf/2004/35450.htm [accessed on 29 December 2004].

70. CTK News Agency (1 December 2005), at www.lexisnexis.com/academic/universe/; *Deutsche Presse-Agentur* (6 December 2005), at www.newsbank.com/govlib/awn; and CTK National News Wire (13 January 2006), at www.lexisnexis.com/academic/universe/.

71. CTK National News Wire (20 July 2005), at www.lexisnexis.com/academic/universe/.

72. Martin Horalek, spokesperson for the Catholic Episcopal Conference, as reported in CTK National News Wire (22 June 2005), at www.lexisnexis.com/academic/universe/.

73. CTK's paraphrase of the views of Czech Catholic bishops, in CTK National News Wire (11 November 2005), at www.lexisnexis.com/academic/universe/.

74. CTK News Agency (1 February 2006), at www.lexisnexis.com/academic/universe/.

75. CTK National News Wire (13 July 2005), CTK National News Wire (6 September 2005), and CTK News Agency (19 December 2005)—all at www.lexisnexis.com/academic/universe/.

76. Quoted in CTK News Agency (16 December 2005), at www.newsbank.com/govlib/awn.

77. CTK News Agency (26 January 2006), at www.newsbank.com/govlib/awn.

78. CTK National News Wire (26 January 2006), at www.lexisnexis.com/academic/universe/.

79. CTK National News Wire (18 February 2006) and CTK News Agency (21 February 2006)—both at www.lexisnexis.com/academic/universe/.

80. According to a survey conducted in October 2005 by the Georg and Focus agencies and reported in *Slovak Spectator* (11 December 2005), at www.newsbank.com/govlib/awn.

81. CTK News Agency, 15 March 2006 and 16 March 2006—both at www.newsbank.com/govlib/awn.

82. Sharon Fisher, "Church Restitution Law Passed in Slovakia," in *RFE/RL Research Report* (19 November 1993), 51–53.

83. Quoted in *Ibid.,* 54.

84. *Slovak Spectator* (15 November 1999), at www.slovakspectator.sk [accessed on 21 October 2004].

85. *Slovak Spectator* (1 February 1999), at www.slovakspectator.sk [accessed on 21 October 2004].

86. *Slovak Spectator* (21 February 1999), at www.slovakspectator.sk [accessed on 21 October 2004].

87. *Prague Post* (30 August 1995), at www.praguepost.com [accessed on 21 October 2004].

88. *Slovak Spectator* (23 November 1998), at www.slovakspectator.sk [accessed on 21 October 2004].

89. *Slovak Spectator* (7 December 1998), at www.slovakspectator.sk [accessed on 21 October 2004].

90. Regarding yoga, see *Slovak Spectator* (16 July 2001), at www.slovakspectator.sk [accessed on 21 October 2004]; and Jonathan Luxmoore, "Slovak Churches Applaud Decision to Drop Plan for Yoga in Schools," in *Christianity Today* (18 October 2001), at www.christianitytoday.com [accessed on 29 December 2004]. Regarding abortion, see *Slovak Spectator* (4 August 2003), at www.slovakspectator.sk [accessed on 21 October 2004]; and *National Catholic Reporter* (12 September 2003), at nationalcatholicreporter.org [accessed on 29 December 2004]. Regarding same-sex unions, see *Slovak Spectator* (22 October 2001), at www.slovakspectator.sk [accessed on 21 October 2004]; slovensko.com, 22 July 2004 and 26 October 2004—both at www.slovensko.com/news [accessed on 26 October 2004].

91. *Slovak Spectator* (5 May 2003), at www.slovakspectator.sk [accessed on 21 October 2004].

92. CTK National News Wire (16 July 2003), at www.lexisnexis.com/academic/universe/.

93. CTK National News Wire (20 January 2004), at www.lexisnexis.com/academic/universe/.

94. Tomas Galis, assistant bishop in Banska Bystrica, as paraphrased in CTK National News Wire (5 March 2003), at www.lexisnexis.com/academic/universe/.

95. Associated Press Worldstream (9 November 2005), at www.lexisnexis.com/academic/universe/.

96. TASR News Agency (Bratislava), 15 July 2002, at www.newsbank.com/govlib/awn. The reference is to the European Parliament's resolution on the subject.

97. *Slovak Spectator* (11 December 2005), at www.newsbank.com/govlib/awn.

98. TASR News Agency (6 February 2001) and TASR News Agency (23 February 2001)—both at www.newsbank.com/govlib/awn.

99. *Slovak Spectator* (15 September 2001), and *Slovak Spectator* (5 May 2003)—both at www.newsbank.com/govlib/awn; and SITA News Agency (Bratislava), 5 September 2003, at www.newsbank.com/govlib/awn.

100. Daniel Lipsic, deputy chair of the KDH and Minister of Justice, as quoted in TASR News Agency (28 July 2003), at www.lexisnexis.com/academic/universe/.

101. Deutsche Presse-Agentur (13 January 2005), at www.newsbank.com/govlib/awn.

102. *Sme* (Bratislava), 28 December 2005, in *BBC Monitoring Europe—Political* (30 December 2005), via www.lexisnexis.com/academic/universe/.

103. CTK National News Wire (6 February 2006), at www.lexisnexis.com/academic/universe/; and *The Guardian* (11 February 2006), at www.guardian.co.uk [accessed on 1 March 2006]. See also website of the Slovak Democratic and Christian Union (7 February 2006), at www.sdkuonline.sk/english/ [accessed on 5 March 2006].

104. *Slovak Spectator* (4 June 2006), at www.newsbank.com/govlib/awn.

105. *Slovak Spectator* (3 November 2003), at www.lexisnexis.com/academic/universe/.

106. CTK National News Wire (20 October 2003), at www.lexisnexis.com/academic/universe/.

107. Deutsche Presse-Agentur (9 November 2005), at www.lexisnexis.com/academic/universe/.

108. Letter from the Slovak Bishops' Conference to Ludovit Kanik, Minister of Labor and Social Affairs, as summarized in CTK National News Wire (12 July 2004), at www.lexisnexis.com/academic/universe/.

109. Ann Burlein, *Lift High the Cross: Where White Supremacy and the Christian Right Converge* (Durham, N.C.: Duke University Press, 2002), 109–10.

CHAPTER SEVEN

As mentioned in the preface, a Serbian translation of an earlier version of this paper was published under the title "Klizanje unazad: Sudbina žena u centralnoj i istočnoj Evropi posle 1989," *Ljudska bezbednost/Human Security* (Belgrade) 1, no. 1 (2003): 115–33. This paper has been presented at the University Residential Center of the University of Bologna, Bertinoro, Italy (7 September 2003), at the Faculty of Political Science, University of Belgrade (8 June 2004), at the Seminar for Democracy and Human Rights, Konjic (14 July 2004), and at the Department for Southeast European History, University of Graz (11 November 2004).

1. Mark Kramer, "Social Protection Policies and Safety Nets in East-Central Europe: Dilemmas of the Postcommunist Transformation," in Ethan B. Kapstein and Michael Mandelbaum, eds., *Sustaining the Transition: The Social Safety Net in Postcommunist Europe* (New York: Council on Foreign Relations, 1997), 46.

2. Brandie Sasser, "Gender and Labor Markets in Transition Countries," paper presented at the Eastern Europe and Central Asia Region conference, Warsaw, Poland, 15–17 January 2001, 4,

3. Ibid., 5.

4. Ibid., 8–9.

5. George L. Mosse, *Nationalism and Sexuality: Middle-Class Morality and Sexual Norms in Modern Europe* (Milwaukee: University of Wisconson Press, 1985).

6. Žarana Papić, "Women in Serbia: Post-Communism, War, and Nationalist Mutations," in Sabrina Ramet, ed., *Gender Politics in the Western Balkans: Women and Society in Yugoslavia and the Yugoslav Successor States* (University Park, Pa.: Pennsylvania State University Press, 1999), 154–55.

7. *Vjesnik* (Zagreb), 15 June 1993, 3.

8. Anto Baković, *Concept for the Demographic and Moral Renewal of Croatia* (May 1992), as quoted in Rada Iveković, "The New Democracy: With Women or Without Them?" in Sabrina Petra Ramet and Ljubiša S. Adamovich, eds., *Beyond Yugoslavia: Politics, Economics, and Culture in a Shattered Community* (Boulder, Colo.: Westview Press, 1995), 400.

9. Belinda Cooper, "Building Feminism from the Ground Up," *Journal* 1, no. 3 (1997), at www.civnet.org/journal/issue3/cfbeco.htm (accessed 11 August 2003), 6.

10. Siniša Stanimirović, "Serbia: Suicide on the Rise," *Institute for War & Peace Reporting*, BCR No. 344 (20 June 2002), at www.iwpr.net (accessed 6 August 2002).

11. Jennifer Friedlin, "Bosnia: Suicides on the Rise," *Institute for War & Peace Reporting*, BCR No. 303 (12 December 2001), at www.iwpr.net (accessed 14 March 2002).

12. UNDP, *Human Development Report 2002*, at www.undp.org/hdr2002 (accessed 6 August 2002), E5–2.

13. "2002: A Year of Uncertainty in the Troubled Balkans," at www .ekathimerini.com/news/content.asp?id=114837 (accessed 6 August 2002, via Google cache), 3.

14. Plamen Kulinski, "2001—A Year of Surprises for the Bulgarians," in *AIM Press*, 13 January 2002, at www.aimpress.ch (accessed 19 August 2002).

15. World Bank figure, as reported in U.S. AID, "Romania" (2001), at www .usaid.gov/country/ee/ro (accessed 6 August 2002), 1.

16. Alison Mutler, "Poverty, Corruption Haunt Romania," AP, 17 February 2002, at www.globalpolicy.org/nations/launder/regions/2002/0217romania.htm (accessed 6 August 2002), 1.

17. The immigrants typically pay between $2,000 and $4,000 to be taken to "Western" Europe; see Paul Cristian Radu, "Romania Tackles Human Traffickers," *International War & Peace Reporting*, BCR No. 357 (9 August 2002), at www.iwpr.net (accessed 18 August 2002).

18. UNDP, *Human Development Report 2002*, at www.undp.org/hdr2002 (accessed 6 August 2002), E5–2.

19. Government of the Republic of Macedonia, *Poverty Reduction Strategy Paper* (interim version) (Skopje, 10 November 2000), 1.

20. On unemployment, see Sylke Viola Schnepf, "Transformations of Gender Relations in Central and Eastern Europe: The Impact of Reform on Gender Equality" (Hamburg, Germany), at www.untj.org/files/reports/ifu-paperGenderin Transistion.pdf (accessed 29 May 2006), 6. On wages, see Anna Pollert, "Gender and Transformation in Central Eastern Europe" (University of Greenwich, London), at www.forba.at/files/news/referate/pollert.pdf (accessed 29 May 2006), 3.

21. Teresa Gutierrez, "UNICEF on East Europe's Women: It's Been Downhill under Capitalism," *Workers' World,* September 22, 1999. At www.hartford-hwp .com/archives/63/322.html (accessed 15 September, 2006).

22. Stana Buchowska, "Trafficking in Women: Breaking the Vicious Cycle," in Marnia Lazreg, ed., *Making the Transition Work for Women in Europe and Central Asia* (New York: World Bank, 2000).

23. "Bridging the Gender Gap in Entrepreneurship in Eastern Europe and CIS," United Nations Economic Commission for Europe, press release 13 June 2003, at www.unece.org/press (accessed 11 August 2003).

24. Laura Brunell, "Cinderella Seeks Shelter: Will the State, Church, or Civil Society Provide?" *East European Politics and Societies* 16, no. 2 (2002): 469.

25. Magdalena Grabowska and Wanda Nowicka, "Attitudes of Rural Women toward Reproduction Issues: Report on the Survey Conducted by RUN," *The Anti-Abortion Law in Poland* (September 2000), at www.waw.pdi.net/~polfedwo/english/reports/report00/repo0_6.htm (accessed 11 August 2003), 3.

26. Cooper, "Building Feminism," 3; and Sabrina Ramet, "In Tito's Time," in Ramet, *Gender Politics*, 101.

27. Gutierrez, "UNICEF on East Europe's Women," 1.

28. Vlasta Jalušič, "Women in Post-Socialist Slovenia: Socially Adapted, Politically Marginalized," in Ramet, *Gender Politics*, 125; and Papić, "Women in Serbia," 164.

29. Vlasta Jalušič and Milica Antić, "Prospects for Gender Equality Policies in Central and Eastern Europe," *Social Costs of Economic Transformation in Central Europe*, SOCO Project Paper No. 79 (Vienna: Institut für die Wissenschaften vom Menschen, 1994), 9–11.

30. Ibid., 7.

31. Contempt for feminism is also associated with a tolerance for sexual harassment. In the Czech Republic, a recent survey found that 45% of Czech women had been victims of sexual harassment, many of them on repeated occasions; see "Sexual Harassment in Central and Eastern Europe," *New York Times*, 9 January 2000, reprinted in *WIN News*, Spring 2000, at www.findarticles.com (accessed 1 September 2003).

32. Magdalena Środa, "Król jest nagi! Niech zyje królowa!" [The king is naked! Long live the queen!], *Oska Biuletin*, No. 2 (2001): 33, as quoted in Joanna Renc-Roe, "The Representation of Women in the Political Decision-Making Process in Poland: Existing Problems and Advocated Solutions," Paper prepared for the ECPR Joint Session: Changing Constitutions, Building Institutions and (Re)defining Gender Relations, Edinburgh, 28 March–2 April 2003, 4.

33. Ibid., 12–14.

34. Human Rights Internet, *For the Record 2001: The United Nations Human Rights System*, vol. 5: *Central and Eastern Europe* (Ottawa: HRI, 2002), 3.

35. "Equal Opportunities: MEPs Vote for More Women in Power," *European Report*, 25 November 2000, at www.findarticles.com (accessed 1 September 2003).

36. "East Central Europe Abortion Laws and Policies in Brief," *Center for Reproductive Rights* (August 2000), at www.crlorg/tools/print_page.jsp (accessed 29 August 2003).

37. Wanda Nowicka and Monika Tajak, "The Functioning, Social Effects, Attitudes and Behaviors—The Report," *The Anti-Abortion Law in Poland*, September 2000, at www.waw.pdi.net/~polfedwo/english/report00/repo0.3.htm (accessed 11 August 2003).

38. Ibid., 3, 6; *Guardian* (London), 20 June 2003 and 23 June 2003, both at www.guardian.co.uk (both accessed 18 July 2003).

39. Nowicka and Tajak, "Functioning, Social Effects," 3, 5

40. Ibid., 7.

41. Buchowska, "Breaking the Vicious Circle," 1.

42. Norbert Mappes-Niedliek, *Balkan Mafia. Staaten in der Hand des Verbrechens—Eine Gefahr für Europa* (Berlin: Ch. Links, 2003), 109–15.

43. Regan E. Ralph, "International Trafficking of Women and Children," Testimony before the Senate Committee on Foreign Relations, Subcommittee on Near Eastern and South Asian Affairs, 22 February 2000, at www.hrw.org/backgrounder/wrd/trafficking.htm (accessed 11 August 2003), 2.

44. Ibid., 3.

45. Ibid.

46. Nicole Lindstrom, "Regional Sex Trafficking in the Balkans: Transnational Networks in an Enlarged Europe," *Problems of Post-Communism* 51, no. 3 (2004): 47. On Britain, Greece, Italy, Germany, and Spain, *Daily Telegraph* (London), 27 November 2005, at www.telegraph.co.uk/ (accessed 2 December 2005). On Austria, Deutsche Presse-Agentur, 28 September 2005; Russia, Basapress (Moldovan news agency), 9 August 2005; Turkey, Basapress, 24 July 2004, all at www.newsbank.com/govlib/awn.

47. "UN Cracks down on Bosnia Prostitution," *BBC News,* 2 November 2001, and "Victims of Bosnia's Sex Trade," *BBC News,* 2 November 2001, both at news.bbc.co.uk (accessed 11 August 2003). See also Peter Andreas, "The Clandestine Political Economy of War and Peace in Bosnia," *International Studies Quarterly* 48 (2004): 29–51.

48. "'Sex Trade' Thrives in Bosnia," *BBC News,* 8 March 2001, at news.bbc.co.uk (accessed 11 August 2003).

49. "Serbian Police Swoop on Vice Bars," *BBC News,* 25 January 2002, at news.bbc.co.uk (accessed 11 August 2003).

50. "Trafficking in Women: European Commission Paper Sets out Priority Actions," *European Report,* 16 December 1998; and "European Parliament Urges Action to Stop Trafficking in Women," *European Report,* 24 May 2000, both at www.findarticles.com (accessed 1 September 2003).

51. "EU 'to Protect' Sex Slaves," *BBC News,* 8 March 2001, at news.bbc.co.uk (accessed 11 August 2003), 1.

52. Buchowska, "Breaking the Vicious Circle," 3.

53. Deutsche Presse-Agentur, 31 March 2005, at www.newsbank.com/govlib/awn.

54. Bosnia-Herzegovina, Onasa News Agency (Sarajevo), 20 June 2003; Moldova, Infotag News Agency (Chisinau), 10 May 2005; Albania, *Rilindja Demokratike* (Tirana), 17 January 2006; Croatia, Serbia, and Bosnia-Herzegovina, HINA (Zagreb), 14 November 2004; Kosovo, HINA, 2 April 2005; and Romania, Rompres News Agency (Bucharest), 9 June 2005—all at www.newsbank.com/govlib/awn.

55. Quoted in Sabrina Ramet, *Social Currents in Eastern Europe: The Sources*

and Consequences of the Great Transformation, 2d ed. (Durham, N.C.: Duke University Press, 1995), 449.

56. *Women 2000: An Investigation into the Status of Women's Rights in Central and South-Eastern Europe and the Newly Independent States* (Vienna: International Helsinki Federation for Human Rights, 2000), 123; and U.S. Department of State, *1999 Country Reports on Human Rights Practices—Croatia,* Released by the Bureau of Democracy, Human Rights, and Labor, 25 February 2000, at www.state.gov/www.global/human_rights/1999_hrp_report/croatia.html, 23.

57. HINA, 9 December 2004, at www.newsbank.com/govlib/awn.

58. *Women 2000,* 421.

59. "Prevalence of Domestic Violence," *Minnesota Advocates for Human Rights,* at www1.umn.edu/humanrts/svaw/domestic/link/statistics.htm (accessed 11 August 2003), 1.

60. Romania, Rompres News Agency, 31 March 2004; Slovakia, *Slovak Spectator* (Bratislava), 2 September 2005 and 9 September 2005, all at www.newsbank.com/govlib/awn.

61. Quoted in *Budapest Sun,* 16 February 2006, at www.budapestsun.com/ (accessed 17 February 2006). Concerning no law against domestic violence, see *Budapest Sun,* 23 September 2004, at www.newsbank.com/govlib/awn.

62. R. I. Moore, *The Formation of a Persecuting Society: Power and Deviance in Western Europe, 950–1250* (Oxford: Basil Blackwell, 1987).

63. Tatjana Pavlović, "Women in Croatia: Feminists, Nationalists, and Homosexuals," in Ramet, *Gender Politics,* 134.

64. "Orthodox Statement on Homosexuality," *Word,* January 1984, at http://www.holy-trinity.org/morality/homosexuality.html (accessed 13 August 2003), 6–11.

65. "The Church is against the Homosexuality: Open Letter of His Beatitude Patriarch Teoctist against the Intention of the Romanian Parliament to Abrogate Article 200 in the Penal Code, concerning the Homosexual Relations," 13 September 2000, at biserica.org/Publicatii/2001?NoX/XII_index.html (accessed 13 August 2003).

66. Otto F. Kernberg, "Hatred as Pleasure," in Robert A. Glick and Stanley Bone, eds., *Pleasure beyond the Pleasure Principle* (New Haven, Conn.: Yale University Press, 1990), 179–80.

67. Martha C. Nussbaum, *Sex and Social Justice* (New York: Oxford University Press, 1999), 190.

68. Martha C. Nussbaum, "Religion and Women's Human Rights," in Paul J. Weithman, ed., *Religion and Contemporary Liberalism* (Notre Dame, Ind.: University of Notre Dame Press, 1997), 134.

69. On the relationship between liberalism and feminism, see Nussbaum, *Sex and Social Justice,* cha 2 ("The Feminist Critique of Liberalism").

70. David Hollenbach, "Afterword: A Community of Freedom," in R. Bruce Douglass and David Hollenbach, eds., *Catholicism and Liberalism: Contributions to American Public Philosophy* (Cambridge: Cambridge University Press, 1994), 333.

71. Gloria Steinem, "What It Would Be Like If Women Win," in Michael E. Adelstein and Jean G. Pival, eds., *Women's Liberation* (New York: St. Martin's Press, 1972), 143.

72. For further discussion of these values, see Vladimir Tismaneanu, "Truth, Trust, Tolerance: Intellectuals in Post-Communist Society," *Problems of Post-Communism* 43, no. 2 (1996).

73. Regarding the debacle produced by America's realist approach to crime fighting, see "Justice in America: Too Many Convicts," *Economist* (London), 10 August 2002, 15.

CHAPTER EIGHT

1. "The Action Program of the Communist Party of Czechoslovakia" (5 April 1968), printed as an appendix to Alexander Dubček, *Hopes Dies Last: The Autobiography of the Leader of the Prague Spring,* ed. and trans. by Jiří Hochman (New York: Kodansha International, 1993), 296.

2. Concerning the Chetniks' collaboration with Axis forces, see Walter Manoschek, *"Serbien ist judenfrei." Militärische Besatzungspolitik und Judenvernichtung in Serbien 1941/42* (Munich: R. Oldenbourg Verlag, 1995); Matteo J. Milazzo, *The Chetnik Movement & the Yugoslav Resistance* (Baltimore: Johns Hopkins University Press, 1975); and Jozo Tomašević, *War and Revolution in Yugoslavia, 1941–1945: Occupation and Collaboration* (Stanford, Calif.: Stanford University Press, 2001).

3. See Sabrina Ramet, "Americanization, Anti-Americanism, and Commercial Aggression against Culture: An Introduction," in Sabrina Ramet and Gordana Crnković, eds., *Kazaaam! Splat! Ploof! American Influences on European Culture, since 1945* (Lanham, Md.: Rowman & Littlefield, 2003).

4. Robyn Eckersley, "Deliberative Democracy, Ecological Representation and Risk: Towards a Democracy of the Affected," in Michael Saward, ed., *Democratic Innovation: Deliberation, Representation and Association* (New York: Routledge, 2000), 119.

5. Amy Gutmann and Dennis Thompson, *Democracy and Disagreement* (Cambridge, Mass.: Belknap Press of Harvard University Press, 1996), 112.

6. Hartmut Krauss, *Faschismus und Fundamentalismus* (Osnabrück: Hintergrund Verlag, 2003), 159.

7. Tor Bukkvoll, "Private Interests, Public Policy: Ukraine and the Common Economic Space Agreement," *Problems of Post-Communism* 51, no. 5 (2004): 14–15.

8. Nenad Čanak, president of the provincial assembly of Vojvodina, in interview with the author, Novi Sad, June 2004.

9. Bianca L. Adair, "Democratization and Regime Transformation in Hungary," *Problems of Post-Communism* 49, no. 2 (2002): 52–53.

10. Jean Bethke Elshtain, *Democracy on Trial* (New York: Basic Books, 1995).

11. See Michael Cromartie, ed., *A Public Faith: Evangelicals and Civic Engagement* (Lanham, Md.: Rowman & Littlefield and the Ethics and Public Policy Center, 2003). See also John C. Green, Mark J. Rozell, and Clyde Wilcox, eds., *The*

Christian Right in American Politics: Marching to the Millennium (Washington D.C.: Georgetown University Press, 2003); and Dale Buss, *Family Man: The Biography of Dr. James Dobson* (Wheaton, Ill.: Tyndale House, 2005).

12. Quoted in Steven Brown, *Trumping Religion: The New Christian Right, the Free Speech Clause, and the Courts* (Tuscaloosa: University of Alabama Press, 2002), 13.

13. Gabriel Bădescu, Paul Sum, and Eric M. Uslaner, "Civil Society Development and Democratic Values in Romania and Moldova," *East European Politics and Societies* 18, no. 2 (2004): 322.

14. For a discussion of corruption in the region, see Rasma Karklins, "Typology of Post-Communist Corruption," *Problems of Post-Communism* 49, no. 4 (2002): 22–32.

15. Michael Johns, "'Do as I Say, Not as I Do': The European Union, Eastern Europe, and Minority Rights," *East European Politics and Societies* 17, no. 4 (2003): 692.

16. Details in Sabrina Ramet, "Church and State in Romania before and after 1989," in Henry F. Carey, ed., *Politics and Society in Post-Communist Romania* (Lanham, Md.: Lexington Books, 2004), 275–95.

17. For discussion, see Sabrina Ramet, "Thy Will Be Done: The Catholic Church and Politics in Poland since 1989," in Timothy A. Byrnes and Peter J. Katzenstein, eds., *Religion in an Expanding Europe* (Cambridge: Cambridge University Press, 2006).

18. "Inter-Orthodox Talks on Draft Constitutional Treaty of European Union," *Novosti,* Information Service of the Serbian Orthodox Church (Belgrade), 4 April 2003, at www.spc.org.yu/Vesti-2003/04/4-4-03_el.html (accessed 13 August 2003), 1–2. See also "Inter-Orthodox Conference in Crete on the Draft Constitutional Treaty of the European Union," *Russian Orthodox Church News* (2003), at www.russian-orthodox-church.org/ru/ne303313.htm (accessed 13 August 2003).

19. See the report in *Victoria Advocate,* 21 June 2003, at victoriaadvocate-proxy.nandomedia.com/Religion/v-print/story/1153325p-1374 (accessed 13 August 2003).

20. *Warsaw Voice,* 31 March 2002, www.lexisnexis.com/academic/universe/.

21. *Warsaw Voice,* 19 May 2002; see also *Polish News Bulletin,* 8 May 2002, both www.lexisnexis.com/academic/universe/.

22. Michael Emerson, "Faith That Separates: Evangelicals and Black-White Race Relations," in Cromartie, *Public Faith,* 188.

23. The concept of reasonableness is given particular stress in John Rawls, *Political Liberalism* (New York: Columbia University Press, 1993, 1996).

24. Richard Rorty, *Philosophy and Social Hope* (London: Penguin Books, 1999), xci–xxi, 28.

25. Richard Rorty, "What Do You Do When They Call You a 'Relativist'?" *Philosophy and Phenomenological Research* 57, no. 1 (1997): 176; Rorty, "Postmodernist Bourgeois Liberalism," *Journal of Philosophy* 80, no. 10, pt. 1 (1983): 587; and Rorty, "Is Truth a Goal of Enquiry? Davidson vs. Wright," *Philosophical Quarterly* 45, no. 180 (1995): 300.

26. Richard Rorty, *Consequences of Pragmatism (Essays: 1972–1980)* (Brighton: Harvester Press, 1982), xiii.

27. See, for example, Jürgen Habermas, *The Inclusion of the Other: Studies in Political Theory,* ed. by Ciaran Cronin and Pablo De Greiff (Cambridge/Oxford: Polity Press and Blackwell Publishers, 1999).

CHAPTER NINE

1. On this debate, see Sabrina Ramet, *Balkan Babel: The Disintegration of Yugoslavia from the Death of Tito to the Fall of Milošević,* 4th ed. (Boulder, Colo.: Westview Press, 2002), chap. 13 ("Milošević, Kosovo, and the Principle of Legitimacy").

2. See Jeffrey W. Legro and Andrew Moravcsik, "Is Anybody Still a Realist?" *International Security* 24, no. 2 (1999).

3. See Vladimir Tismaneanu's revealing preface to *Reinventing Politics: Eastern Europe from Stalin to Havel* (New York: Free Press, 1992). See also Tismaneanu, ed., *In Search of Civil Society: Independent Peace Movements in the Soviet Bloc* (New York: Routledge, 1990); and Anonymous, *From Below: Independent Peace and Environmental Movements in Eastern Europe and the USSR* (New York: Helsinki Watch, October 1987).

4. See details and documentation in Sabrina Ramet, *Social Currents in Eastern Europe: The Sources and Consequences of the Great Transformation,* 2d ed. (Durham, N.C.: Duke University Press, 1995), cha 1.

5. "Marta Toch," *Reinventing Civil Society: Poland's Quiet Revolution, 1981–1986* (New York: Helsinki Watch, December 1986).

6. Quoted in the HDZ newspaper, *Državnost,* as cited in *Feral Tribune,* 22 December 1995, trans. in Mark Thompson, *Forging War: The Media in Serbia, Croatia, Bosnia and Hercegovina,* 2d ed. (Luton: University of Luton Press, 1999), 356, punctuation modified.

7. Chris Brown, "Introduction," in Chris Brown, ed., *Political Restructuring in Europe: Ethical Perspectives* (New York: Routledge, 1994), 3–4.

8. Thomas W. Pogge, "Cosmopolitanism and Sovereignty," in Brown, *Political Restructuring in Europe,* 99.

9. Alan Gewirth, *Reason and Morality* (Chicago: University of Chicago Press, 1978); and Gewirth, *The Community of Rights* (Chicago: University of Chicago Press, 1996).

10. See, for example, the following books by Jürgen Habermas, all published by MIT Press in Cambridge, Mass.: *Moral Consciousness and Communicative Action,* trans. from German by Christian Lenhartdt and Shierry Weber Nicholsen (1990); *Between Facts and Norms: Contributions to a Discourse Theory of Law and Democracy,* trans. from German by William Rehg (1996); and *The Inclusion of the Other: Studies in Political Theory,* ed. by Ciaran Cronin and Pablo De Greif (1998).

11. Susan Mendus, ed., *Justifying Toleration: Conceptual and Historical Perspectives* (Cambridge: Cambridge University Press, 1988); and Mendus, ed., *The Politics of Toleration in Modern Life* (Durham, N.C.: Duke University Press, 2000).

NOTES TO PAGE 126   **155**

12. John Rawls, *Political Liberalism* (New York: Columbia University Press, 1993, 1996); and John Rawls, *The Law of Peoples* (Cambridge, Mass.: Harvard University Press, 1999).

13. Joseph Raz, *The Morality of Freedom* (Oxford: Clarendon Press, 1986).

14. Ian Shapiro, *The Moral Foundations of Politics* (New Haven, Conn.: Yale University Press, 2003).

15. For a more detailed expostulation, see Sabrina Ramet, *Whose Democracy? Nationalism, Religion, and the Doctrine of Collective Rights in Post-1989 Eastern Europe* (Lanham, Md.: Rowman & Littlefield, 1997), introduction, chap. 3, conclusion.

16. Barry Hindess, "Liberalism, Socialism and Democracy: Variations on a Governmental Theme," in Andrew Barry, Thomas Osborne, and Nikolas Rose, eds., *Foucault and Political Reason: Liberalism, Neo-liberalism and Rationalities of Government* (Chicago: University of Chicago Press, 1996), 67.

BIBLIOGRAPHIC ESSAY

The starting point, if one wishes to understand either the intersection of morality and politics or the moral foundation of political legitimacy, is Immanuel Kant. Not all of Kant's work is immediately comprehensible, but among the more accessible and also critical works one may mention his *Grundlegung zur Metaphysik der Sitten,* translated into English by H. J. Paton under the title *Groundwork of the Metaphysic of Morals* (New York: Harper & Row, 1964), and Kant's later and fuller work, *Metaphysik der Sitten,* translated into English by Mary Gregor under the title *The Metaphysics of Morals* (Cambridge, Cambridge University Press, 1996). In the former work, Kant restricts himself to establishing what he considers to be the fundamental principle of morality, the categorical imperative, which counsels that moral choices must pass the test of universalizability. In the latter work, Kant develops his moral theory more fully, explaining its connections with politics. In these works, Kant lays special stress on the duty of truthfulness (although he recognizes that this duty may be suspended in the interest of common courtesy or— one must imagine—also in the exercise of obvious comedy). While Kant's work is well known by reputation, I suspect that it is too often honored in neglect rather than in study and reflection.

Kant's influence is pervasive, and such major figures in contemporary ethical philosophy as Alan Gewirth, Jürgen Habermas, and John Rawls all continue, in one way or another, Kant's legacy. Gewirth occupies a unique niche in this pantheon, having endeavored no less than to accomplish what he believes no other ethicist, Kant included, had accomplished, namely, to demonstrate the rational grounds for morality. This question—Why should I be moral?—lies at the foundation of Gewirth's monumental *Reason and Morality* (Chicago, University of Chicago Press, 1978). Like Kant, Gewirth offers us a supreme principle of morality, his Principle of Generic Consistency: "Act in accord with the generic rights of your recipients as well as yourself." And like Kant, Gewirth suggests that all other moral principles and imperatives can be derived from this first principle. But Gewirth also sees his formula as an improvement upon that of Kant and argues that it cannot be challenged without self-contradiction, with the result that criminals are not merely rule breakers but are, also, ipso facto, illogical.

Among other political thinkers of more recent times, there are several whose work I find especially useful. Habermas's *The Inclusion of the Other: Studies in Political Theory* (Cambridge, Mass.: MIT Press, 1998) offers an articulate defense of Kantian liberalism, updating it and applying it to contemporary problems and challenges. Rawls's *Political Liberalism* (New York: Columbia University Press, 1996), while likewise reflecting Kant's influence, invites readers to imagine how they would design a system if they could not be sure what position they would occupy in it; the conclusion is that, under such conditions, people would be intent on designing a system that would protect its poor, its sick, its aged members, and, as well, a system that would enshrine liberal principles.

In the field of contemporary political philosophy, one cannot avoid the names L. W. Sumner, J. W. Harris, Joseph Raz, Susan Mendus, and Will Kymlicka. Sumner's *The Moral Foundation of Rights* (Oxford: Clarendon Press, 1987) shows that rights are grounded in morality, with the result that differences in moral concept make for differences in one's concept of rights. Sumner outlines the four philosophical theories about morality—universalism, conventionalism, consequentialism, and contractarianism. Thus, for example, if one is a conventionalist and believes that what is right and wrong is only what is determined by law and written convention, then it follows that one believes that one has rights only insofar as they are sanctioned by law or written agreement.

J. W. Harris is perhaps best known for his *Law and Legal Science: An Inquiry into the Concepts Legal Rule and Legal System* (Oxford: Clarendon Press, 1979), in which he investigates theories of law, offering his thoughts on legal structure and legal validity. Oxford scholar Joseph Raz's *The Morality of Freedom* (Oxford: Clarendon Press, 1986) is an ambitious endeavor to sort out the nature of rights, duties, values, and the justification of political authority. In the process, Raz reinterprets the liberal tradition, arguing for a perfectionistic moral pluralism. Susan Mendus, a professor of politics at the University of York, has made major contributions to our understanding of the nature and importance of tolerance. Of her books I mention two edited volumes: *Justifying Toleration: Conceptual and Historical Perspectives* (Cambridge: Cambridge University Press, 1988), and *The Politics of Toleration in Modern Life* (Durham, N.C.: Duke University Press, 2000). Both volumes argue that toleration, limited only by the harm principle (which is to say, one should tolerate everything that is not harmful), is an essential and integral part of the liberal tradition broadly conceived.

Then there is Will Kymlicka, a professor of philosophy at Queen's University, who has undertaken to revise the liberal tradition to incorporate a concept of special cultural rights within fixed territories. Kymlicka is fully aware that, traditionally, liberalism has emphasized individual rights and equality, but he argues that such an approach can threaten the survival of minority cultures. The solution, he argues at length in *Multicultural Citizenship: A Liberal Theory of Minority Rights* (Oxford: Oxford University Press, 1995), as well as elsewhere, is to broaden the liberal theory of rights to recognize cultural or group rights. In his concept, such rights would include the right of cultural minorities to restrict the rights, and qualify the equality, of members of the majority nationality within their territories. Will Kymlicka also coedited a volume with Ian Shapiro in which diverse views are brought together: *Ethnicity and Group Rights* (New York: New York University Press, 1997).

There is a large literature on secession, but one work which, with time, seems ever more obviously to command the field is Allen Buchanan's *Secession: The Morality of Political Divorce from Fort Sumter to Lithuania and Quebec* (Boulder, Colo.: Westview Press, 1991). Buchanan challenges simplified approaches to the question of secession, arguing that self-determination need not require sovereignty, but outlines conditions in which a state forfeits its title over seceding territory. His three conditions are failure of the state to protect the people living in that region from physical threats, discriminatory treatment by the state of the people in that region or the perpetration of injustices against those people, and the failure or refusal of the state to protect a group's culture.

Concerning the transition from communism to pluralism in Eastern Europe, I am especially fond of Vladimir Tismaneanu's *Reinventing Politics: Eastern Europe from Stalin to Havel* (New York: Free Press, 1992), which underlines the importance of dissident intellectuals in bringing about the downfall of communism. To this one may add Václav Havel's statement about the importance of integrity, "The Power of the Powerless," which is included in his collection *The Power of the Powerless: Citizens against the State in Central-Eastern Europe* (Armonk, N.Y.: M. E. Sharpe, 1985), and the short *Reinventing Civil Society: Poland's Quiet Revolution, 1981–1986* (New York: Helsinki Watch, 1986), which shows how the parallel society being constructed in Poland in the early 1980s was already beginning the process of bringing down communism in Poland. It is a pity that some observers of the region failed to notice this important publication at the time. And, finally, I may mention my own *Social Currents in Eastern Europe: The Sources and Consequences of the Great Transformation*, 2d ed. (Durham, N.C.: Duke University Press, 1995); based on an extensive reading of samizdat materials and other materials, this book outlines the growth of dissent and parallel society in Eastern Europe in the 1980s, highlighting the role of underground Solidarity in Poland and independent activism in Czechoslovakia, Hungary, and Romania while exploring the political role of rock music and the appearance of new religious movements in the region, among other things.

The classic treatment of gender issues in communist Eastern Europe is probably still *Women, State, and Party in Eastern Europe*, edited by Sharon L. Wolchik and Alfred G. Meyer (Durham, N.C.: Duke University Press, 1985). If there is a new "classic" dealing with women in postcommunist conditions, it is probably Marilyn Rueschemeyer's edited collection, *Women in the Politics of Postcommunist Eastern Europe*, rev. ed. (Armonk, N.Y.: M. E. Sharpe, 1998). Among the first works published on the subject after the fall of communism is Barbara Einhorn's *Cinderella Goes to Market: Citizenship, Gender, and Women's Movements in East Central Europe* (New York: Verso, 1993), which explores how women have coped with the social and economic changes that have accompanied the political transformations in the region. Einhorn also argues convincingly that the revived patriarchal attitudes in Eastern Europe are inextricably interwoven with conservative nationalism. Shana Penn undertook extensive fieldwork with numerous interviews to write her *Solidarity's Secret: The Women Who Defeated Communism in Poland* (Ann Arbor: University of Michigan Press, 2005), showing both the crucial role played by women in the Solidarity underground and the willingness of men to forget women's vital contribution. Wanda Nowicka's *The Anti-abortion Law in Poland: The Functioning, Social Effects, Attitudes and Behaviors,* published in Warsaw by the Federation for Woman and Family Planning (2000), is based on a network unique to the Federation and reflects its author's conviction that the law has had damaging effects on Polish women.

Concerning Church and state in Eastern Europe in general and in Poland and Czechoslovakia (Czech Republic and Slovakia) in particular, the old classic is still Trevor Beeson's *Discretion and Valour: Religious Conditions in Russia and Eastern Europe* (Philadelphia, Fortress Press, 1982); benefiting from input from a large circle of experts, Beeson focuses on the communist era. So too does Janice Broun in her *Conscience and Captivity: Religion in Eastern Europe* (Washington, D.C.: Ethics & Public Policy Center, 1988), for which Grazyna Sikorska contributed a chapter on Poland. Writing a few years later, Paul Mojzes included the early postcommunist years in his *Religious Liberty in Eastern Europe and the USSR: Before and after the Great Transformation* (Boulder, Colo.: East European Monographs, 1992). My own *Nihil Obstat: Religion, Politics, and Social Change in East-Central Europe and Russia* (Durham, N.C.: Duke University Press, 1998) reaches deep into the past to tell its story but concentrates on the twentieth century, especially the years since 1945.

When it comes to scholarly studies of Poland and the Czech and Slovak lands, there are few book-length treatments of the latter but quite a number that deal with Poland. Ludvik Němec's *Church and State in Czechoslovakia* (New York: Vantage Press, 1955) is a flawed but nonetheless valuable work that reflects the horror that the author, a Catholic monsignor, felt for communism. The best known treatment of the Catholic Church's role in the politics of communist Poland is Bogdan Szajkowski's *Next to God . . . Poland: Politics and Religion in Contemporary Poland* (New York: St. Martin's Press, 1983). An alternative treatment is Ronald C. Monticone's *The Catholic Church in Communist Poland 1945–1985: Forty Years of Church-State Relations* (Boulder, Colo.: East European Monographs, 1986). Between these two, Szajkowski is probably stronger on analysis, while Monticone is stronger on details. To these one may add Ronald Modras's *The Catholic Church and Antisemitism: Poland, 1933–1939* (Chur, Switz.: Harwood Academic Publishers, 1994), Hanna Diskin's *The Seeds of Triumph: Church and State in Gomulka's Poland* (Budapest: Central European University Press, 2001), and Adam Michnik's *The Church and the Left,* edited and translated from Polish by David Ost (Chicago: University of Chicago Press, 1992). The last of these is a plea for reconciliation between the anticommunist left and the Catholic Church.

Finally, to this literature one might add Samuel P. Huntington's *Political Order in Changing Societies* (New Haven, Conn.: Yale University Press, 1968), a brilliant defense of the realist position and a veritable tour de force which, in some aspects, argues precisely the opposite of what I have argued in this book.

INDEX

You have issues with sticking to a plan? I've got you!
We have no shortage of books that walk you through the whys of weight loss. However, we do have a shortage of books that offer the hows. In order to lose weight and achieve your health goals, you need a supportive team and someone to walk you through the plan, step by step. Before finishing this book, you will know how to fit the ideas into your daily life, and you will succeed!

You'll form habits so that you can trust your body again.
This book applies the practical principles from positive psychology research to ensure your success. By the end of this book, you will not only look different but also think differently about your body. People report being more optimistic, happier, and more confident. They achieve goals without battling fickle willpower, find their own habit-forming strides, and come to trust in their bodies again

YOU CAN TOO!